IMMIGRATION POLICY

AND THE CHALLENGE OF GLOBALIZATION

IMMIGRATION POLICY AND THE CHALLENGE OF GLOBALIZATION

UNIONS AND EMPLOYERS IN UNLIKELY ALLIANCE

JULIE R. WATTS

ILR Press, an imprint of

Cornell University Press

ITHACA AND LONDON

First published 2002 by Cornell University Press

Printed in the United States of America

Library of Congress Cataloging-in-Publication Data

Watts, Julie R. (Julie Renée), 1970–
    Immigration policy and the challenge of globalization : unions and employers in unlikely alliance / Julie R. Watts.
        p.   cm.
Includes bibliographical references and index.
    ISBN 0-8014-3938-8 (cloth : alk. paper)
    1. Emigration and immigration—Government policy.   2. Alien labor.
3. Labor unions.   I. Title.
    JV6271 .W38 2001
    325'.1'0905—dc21   2001003847

Cornell University Press strives to use environmentally responsible suppliers and materials to the fullest extent possible in the publishing of its books. Such materials include vegetable-based, low-VOC inks and acid-free papers that are recycled, totally chlorine-free, or partly composed of nonwood fibers. For further information, visit our website at www.cornellpress.cornell.edu.

Cloth printing   10 9 8 7 6 5 4 3 2 1

To Mike

Contents

Acknowledgments

This book was made possible by the many labor union leaders, employer representatives, and government officials who were willing to discuss their positions on immigration and immigration policy openly with me.

I am grateful to Martin Schain for his guidance throughout my graduate studies at New York University and for reading and commenting on numerous drafts of this manuscript. Similarly, Christopher Mitchell and Josep M. Colomer critiqued early drafts and gave me invaluable advice on field research techniques. I would also like to thank David Denoon, Aristide Zolberg, Wayne Cornelius, Marc Rosenblum, Jim Piazza, and David Andrews for their many helpful suggestions.

In Madrid, I benefited from the resources of the Juan March Institute and from the many contacts of the resourceful Martha Peach. During my stay in Paris, Patrick Weil provided me with working space and helped me to connect with several informants.

I am grateful to Fran Benson at Cornell University Press for recognizing the importance of this research and for making suggestions that improved the manuscript. Moreover, reviewers and editors at *Policy Studies Journal*, *South European Society and Politics* and the Center for Comparative Immigration Studies at the University of California, San

Diego, provided helpful comments before publishing excerpts of the work.

Finally, I am indebted to my husband, Mike, whose advice, patience, and support sustained me through five years of research and writing.

JULIE R. WATTS

Los Angeles, California

Abbreviations

ACLP	Alvarez, Cheibub, Limongi, and Przeworski World Political/Economic Database
AFL-CIO	American Federation of Labor-Congress of Industrial Organizations
AEA	American Electronics Association
ANOLF	L'Associazione Nazionale oltre le Frontiere
CCOO	Comisiones Obreras
CENSIS	Centro Studi Investimenti Sociali
CEOE	Confederación Española de Organizaciones Empresariales
CEVIPOF	Centre d'Etude de la Vie Politique Française
CFDT	Confédération Française Démocratique du Travail
CGIL	Confederazione Generale Italiana del Lavoro
CGT	Confédération Générale du Travail
CISL	Confederazione Italiana Sindicati Lavoratori
CITE	Centro de Información para Trabajadores Extranjeros
CNEL	Consiglio Nazionale dell'Economia e del Lavoro
CNIPI	Conseil National pour l'Intégration des Populations Immigrés
CNPF	Conseil National de Patronat Français
CNRS	Centre National de Recherche Scientifique

ETUC	European Trade Union Confederation
EU	European Union
EWIC	Essential Workers Immigration Coalition
FAS	Fond d'Action Sociale
FN	Front National
FO	Force Ouvriére
GDP	Gross Domestic Product
HERE	Hotel Employees and Restaurant Employees International Union
INA	Immigration and Nationality Act
INSEE	Institut National de la Statistique et des Etudes Economiques
IRCA	Immigration Reform and Control Act
IRES	Istituto Ricerche Economiche e Sociali
ITAA	Information Technology Association of America
LOE	Ley Orgánica de Extranjeria
NLRB	National Labor Relations Board
OCRIEST	Office Central pour la Répression de l'Immigration Irrégulière et de l'Emploi sans Titres
OECD	Organization for Economic Cooperation and Development
OMI	Office des Migrations Internationales
ONI	Office National d'Immigration
RAW	Replenishment Agricultural Worker
SAW	Special Agricultural Worker
SCRIP	Select Commission on Immigration and Refugee Policy
SEIU	Service Employees International Union
SIA	Semiconductor Industry Association
SME	Small and Medium Sized Enterprise
UAGA	Unión Almeriense de Ganaderos e Agricultores
UFW	United Farm Workers of America
UGT	Unión General de Trabajadores
UIL	Unione Italiana de Lavoro
UNICE	Union of Industry Confederations and Employers of Europe
UNITE	Union of Needletrades and Industrial Textile Employees
UNITI	Unione Italiana Immigrati

IMMIGRATION POLICY

AND THE CHALLENGE OF GLOBALIZATION

1

How Globalization Makes Unlikely Allies
of Business and Labor

In the mid-1960s, facing substantial and uncontrolled immigration, the leadership of the largest French labor union, the Confédération Générale du Travail (CGT) reiterated its restrictive position on immigration at its 35th Congress:

> This massive entry of labor, which suffers all sorts of discrimination with regard to wages, social benefits, living conditions and trade union rights, is intended to "loosen the labor market." In other words, to organize unemployment and permit the bosses to more easily resist the demands of the working class. (Castles and Kosack 1973, 134)

This view reflects a conventional wisdom common in the twentieth century: that unions oppose immigration for fear that foreign workers will undercut the wages and working conditions of natives. But on the eve of the twenty-first century, many labor union leaders began to challenge this conventional wisdom and support more open immigration policies.

Why would labor leaders adopt a position on immigration that seemingly undermines their domestic constituency? For decades, unions have faced the dilemma of whether to protect local interests or attempt to represent all workers worldwide. For example, American labor leader Eugene Debs wrote in 1910: "The alleged advantages that would come to the Socialist movement because of such heartless exclusion [of immigrants] would all be swept away a thousand times if it placed upon itself a record of barring its doors against the very races most in need of relief" (Debs 1910).

Nonetheless, labor unions' more practical and immediate goals are to secure the highest wages and best employment conditions for their members, which suggests that labor leaders should favor restrictive immigration policies which protect native workers against an influx of cheap, unorganized immigrant labor. Samuel Gompers, a founding father of the American labor movement, wrote in 1911: "Most reluctantly the lines have been drawn by America's workingmen against the indiscriminate admission of aliens to this country. It is simply a case of the self-preservation of the American working class" (Gompers 1911).

But the economic and political conditions that once encouraged labor leaders to adopt a restrictive immigration stance have changed indelibly. Since the 1970s, globalization has challenged state capacity to control immigration, diminished the competitiveness of highly regulated labor markets, and threatened traditional union organization. Today, many labor leaders see immigration as an inevitable consequence of globalization and believe restrictive immigration policies cannot stop the flow of immigrant workers. In fact, many labor leaders in Western Europe and the United States have come to believe that restrictive policies do little more than force immigrants into a precarious legal and economic position, which ultimately undermines the wages and working conditions of all workers. As a result, most labor leaders today favor policies that promote, rather than restrict, immigration. For example, Spanish and Italian labor leaders, who believe their underground economies are a magnet for illegal immigration, support employment-based immigration quotas as an alternative to illegal immigration and as a means to regulate the underground economy. This brings them into an unlikely alliance, at least on this issue, with employers who long have been counted as their chief adversaries.

These findings are based on interviews with Spanish, Italian, and French labor leaders and employers conducted in 1996 and 1997. Even more recently, American labor leaders also have come to appreciate the effects that globalization has had on their long-standing preferences about immigration policy. As a result, the AFL-CIO reversed its stance on amnesty and employer sanctions in February 2000. But although the leadership of the AFL-CIO has changed its position on immigration in line with the European experience, American unions have not yet had time to influence immigration policy. In contrast, the Spanish, Italian, and French unions have been important actors in the immigration policy-making process for many years. For these reasons, incorporating a full analysis of the U.S. case with the Spanish, Italian, and French cases would be premature.

Spanish, Italian, and French labor leaders have been successfully translating their immigration preferences into policy by lobbying for legislation that facilitates legal immigration and improves the situation of immigrant workers. For example, Italian labor unions won a "sponsored" quota policy in a 1998 immigration law that permits unions, and other nongovernmental organizations, to bring immigrants to Italy.[1] Likewise, Spanish labor unions have advocated successfully for increases in annual employment-based immigration quotas to accommodate more legal immigration. These union activities stand the conventional wisdom on its head, placing labor leaders in an unconventional, tacit alliance with employers.

Not surprisingly, most employers share a fundamental belief that firms should be allowed to hire the most qualified workers, regardless of their country of origin. In the United States, individual companies and employer groups actively lobby for more legal immigration and fewer restrictions on hiring practices. However, the Spanish, Italian, and French national employers' associations refrain from taking an active position on immigration policy. Many European employers believe the policy-making process often fails to encompass "company" concerns as increasingly complex and politicized debates focus on the social and political integration of immigrants and border control, which do not directly affect profits and losses. Moreover, unemployment rates close to 12 percent in Italy and France, and 15 percent in Spain, make a public pro-immigration stance politically unsavory for employers. So at

---

[1] Italy's sponsored immigration quota was first implemented in 2000. Of a total 63,000 visas, 15,000 were allocated to the sponsored quota (author interview, Angelo Masetti, National Representative for Migration, UIL, November 28, 2000).

the national level, European employers' public stance on immigration seems ambiguous in light of their philosophically supportive position.

Although business and labor leaders have found some common ground concerning immigration policy, they arrived at their views for quite different reasons. Employers want access to a larger labor pool that includes more flexible immigrant workers. Unions want to improve the legal and employment status of immigrants so that employers cannot hire "precarious" immigrants to undercut the wages and working conditions of native workers; many labor leaders believe that restrictive immigration policies ultimately hurt both immigrant and native workers. In Europe, unions have taken the lead in this alliance on immigration policy and have been influential in gaining amnesties for illegal immigrants, extending work permits, reducing restrictions on family reunification, improving workplace rights for immigrants, and, in Spain and Italy, increasing employment-based immigration quotas. In the United States, employers have dominated the policy-making process, lobbying to increase, or at least maintain, immigration quotas. Recently, however, U.S. labor leaders and employers have begun to discuss possible common interests and have united in support of legislation that would facilitate family reunification, increase permanent employment-based immigration, and legalize undocumented immigrants.

Although unions and employers are key actors in the immigration policy-making process, scant analytical research has been done on their preferences.[2] This void can be attributed, at least in part, to the conventional wisdom that labor opposes immigration in an effort to protect native workers' wages. In this book I demonstrate that this conventional wisdom is wrong, and, further, show how labor unions have used their influence to help moderate immigration policy.

Globalization and the Convergence-Divergence Debate

On an aggregate level, globalization helps explain the convergence of labor leaders' and employers' immigration policy preferences and pol-

---

[2] The only author to develop a systematic argument about why unions prefer more open immigration policies as a result of globalization is Leah Haus (1995).

icy outcomes across countries. For example, Hollifield (1992) describes a convergence of immigration policies among industrialized democracies in the 1960s, 1970s, and early 1980s based on a common understanding of rights-based liberalism and the globalization of markets. Likewise, Cornelius, Martin, and Hollifield (1994) argue that the confluence of rights-based liberalism and changes in international political economy has led to a convergence of policies for controlling immigration among industrialized, labor-importing countries.

My research indicates, however, that domestic political, institutional, and economic factors are crucial intervening variables that affect labor leaders' and employers' immigration preferences and their tactics for influencing policy. Similarly, Collinson (1994) and Baldwin-Edwards (1991) argue that immigration policy convergence in Europe is limited by domestic factors such as national immigration histories, different labor market needs and stages of economic development, and varying degrees of administrative centralization of immigration controls.

Although at first glance immigration policy outcomes in Spain, Italy, and France support the convergence hypothesis, closer examination of specific measures, such as legalization and quotas, reveals distinct preferences and policy outcomes that result from domestic political, economic, and institutional conditions.

Globalization helps shape labor leaders' and employers' immigration preferences by facilitating migration through improvements in transportation and communication technology. Changes in the global economy also have increased the demand for cheap, flexible immigrant workers in labor-intensive sectors such as hotel and restaurant services, seasonal agriculture, construction, and textiles. Ultimately, states that attempt to restrict immigration conflict with market forces. Although states may successfully limit legal immigration, global migration networks help sustain clandestine immigration flows, thus weakening the potency of restrictive policies. As a result, many labor leaders increasingly see immigration as an inevitable consequence of globalization and believe efforts to restrict it will fail.

Changes in the global economy also have affected employers' policy preferences. In the 1950s and 1960s, the system of mass production—based on semi-skilled labor, assembly-line production, and economies of scale—dominated industrial organization in several European countries. During this period, demand for immigrant labor was concentrated in large manufacturing firms, which wielded considerable power at the national level. In the late 1970s and 1980s, technological advances and global economic competition lessened the importance of mass production systems. To increase profitability, many employers experimented with flexible and decentralized employment and production strategies, such as part-time and temporary contracts, and subcontracting to small enterprises. Other employers moved production to the underground economy, where labor costs are lower and labor regulations and unions can be evaded. Today, the demand for immigrant labor is still pervasive. But it is highly decentralized in secondary sectors, such as agriculture and domestic service, and in the underground economy.

If globalization causes the immigration preferences of labor union leaders and employers to converge, then my argument supports an "open polity" analysis. Proponents of the open polity analysis, such as Milner (1988), Ohmae (1990, 1996), and Rogowski (1989), argue that in states exposed to the global economy, group preferences converge because the effects of globalization are uniform across countries. This analysis is relevant to my research because in aggregate economic terms, the Spanish, French, and Italian economies have become increasingly exposed to global competition (see Figure 1).

The open-polity analysis also predicts that policy outcomes should be similar because they are shaped by pluralistic competition among groups whose influence is weighted by their market power (Garrett and Lange 1995). And Figure 2 demonstrates that in the 1990s, immigration policies in Spain, Italy, and France have converged.[3]

How Domestic Institutions Shape Immigration Preferences and Policies

Global economic changes explain the broad convergence of immigration policies in Spain, Italy, and France. However, a closer comparative

[3] I use here the system I develop in detail in Chapter 2, in which 1 represents the most restrictive policy and 5 the most open. Specific policies considered include quotas, family reunification, legalization, and work permits.

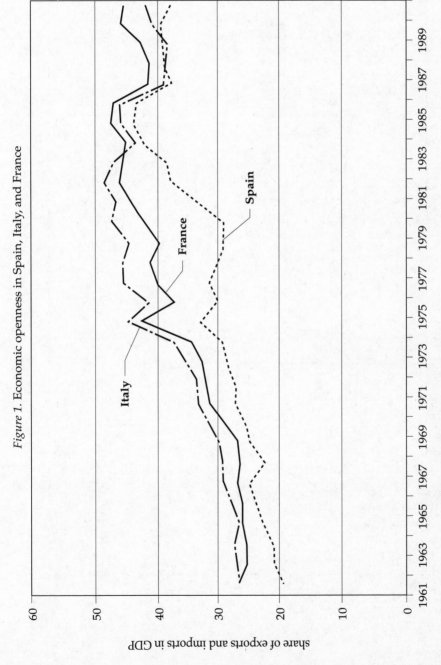

Figure 1. Economic openness in Spain, Italy, and France

share of exports and imports in GDP

Italy

France

Spain

Source: ACLP World Political/Economic database (1995)

7

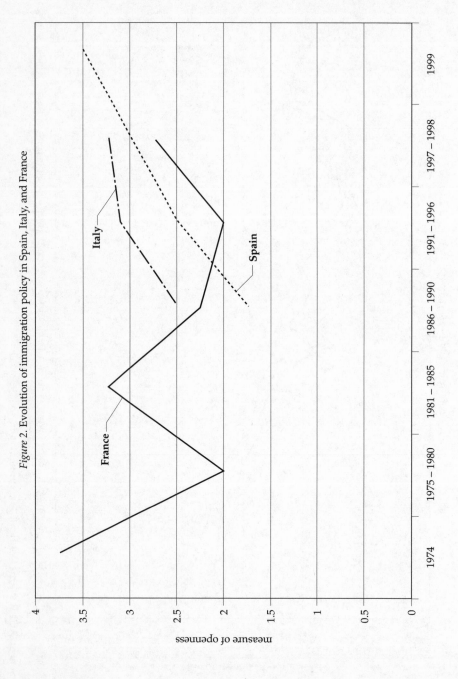

Figure 2. Evolution of immigration policy in Spain, Italy, and France

8

analysis of labor leaders' and employers' immigration policy preferences, as well as details of policy outcomes, reveals that domestic politics, institutions, and economic conditions interact with global economic
changes to shape both preferences and outcomes in distinct ways.

Labor leaders' immigration policy preferences are shaped by domestic factors such as union organization, the institutionalization of private
and governmental immigrant service networks, and the size of the underground economy. For example, because the underground economy
is much larger in Spain and Italy than in France, Spanish and Italian
labor leaders strongly support legalizing illegal immigrants. In contrast, their French counterparts support legalization only for humanitarian reasons.

Also, labor leaders' tactics for influencing the policy-making process
are shaped by domestic factors including whether the right or the left
controls the majority in parliament and whether the Ministry of Labor
or the Ministry of the Interior has authority over the policy-making
process. When the governing majority is conservative, often labor leaders are excluded from the process. As a result, unions must resort to
protest as a means to influence policy outcomes. On the other hand,
leftist governments are more likely to consult with labor leaders because they depend on union support for electoral success. Under these
circumstances, unions have greater opportunity for positive policy
input through formal and informal contacts with policy-makers.

For employers, distinct national labor regulations influence strategies for increasing employment flexibility and determine demand for
immigrant labor. In addition, employer preferences differ between the
national and local levels owing to the decentralization of demand for
immigrant labor. In Spain, for instance, unemployment benefits for seasonal agricultural workers, guaranteed under a 1997 law, have had a
peculiar effect on the immigration situation in the province of Almería,
where the favorable climate permits crops to be grown year-round.
Spanish workers in Almería have the legal right to collect the seasonal
subsidy and not work for three months a year, and they often choose to
stay home during the summer to avoid the intense heat. As a result,
agricultural employers face acute labor shortages during those summer months, and employers' associations in Almería have pressured
the local government to increase the provincial immigration quota.

Several arguments within the divergence debate buttress my thesis that domestic institutions intervene in global economic changes to produce distinct immigration preferences and policy outcomes. These arguments can be divided into three main subsets. The first concerns changes in production models. The second deals with changes in industrial relations. And the third explores divergence in union density rates.

Appelbaum and Batt (1994), Harrison (1994), Locke, Kochan, and Piore (1995), Piore and Sabel (1984), Regini (1995), and Wood (1989) examine how globalization has weakened the system of mass production, and these authors describe alternative production models that have emerged to challenge it. These models include Italian "flexible specialization," Japanese "lean production," and German "diversified quality production."

This body of literature sheds light on how employer demand for immigrant labor in France has shifted since the late 1960s. In the 1950s and 1960s, many large French firms' profitability depended on the availability of semi-skilled immigrant labor. Consequently, the French employers' association, the Conseil National de Patronat Français (CNPF), was a key proponent of open immigration policies. Today immigrants are no longer crucial to the profitability of large French firms, which dominate the CNPF at the national level. In the new decentralized, flexible production model, demand for immigrant labor is concentrated in small firms that can more easily avoid labor laws and union organization. This decentralization of demand, combined with the politicization of French immigration policy, has changed the CNPF's immigration policy preferences at the national level. CNPF leadership no longer sees immigration as a "company" concern and does not publicly support laissez-faire immigration policies.

A second subset of the literature on globalization and economic changes, which includes Crouch and Baglioni (1990), Jacoby (1995), and Regini (1995), investigates the effects of globalization on industrial relations, including collective bargaining, employment relations, and corporatist interest intermediation. According to these authors, globalization forced national systems of industrial relations to undergo profound changes in the 1970s and 1980s. They argue, however, that evidence of convergence in the organization of industrial relations is unclear because the effects of globalization are mediated by national institutions.

Changing institutional and political relationships between the state, business, and labor are important factors in explaining the tactics used by labor leaders to influence the immigration policy-making process. For instance, beginning in the mid-1980s, authority for the immigration policy-making process gradually shifted in Europe from Ministries of Labor to Ministries of the Interior, a result of increasing regionalization and globalization that threatens the ability of European Union member states to control their borders against illegal immigration. In addition, the creation of intergovernmental agreements emphasizing the security and policing aspects of immigration control have given the Ministries of the Interior increasing authority over immigration policy at the expense of Ministries of Labor. As a result, labor unions have less ability to influence policy through their long-term, informal contacts with their Ministry of Labor. Consequently, some unions are devoting resources to organizing and formulating their immigration interests at the European level through the European Trade Union Confederation (ETUC).

A third subset of the literature concerning how globalization affects economic relations explores changes in union density rates. Hyman (1994), Lange and Scruggs (1998), Visser (1991), and Western (1997) conclude that globalization is not causing union membership to decline uniformly across countries. Although these authors agree that globalization may have a deleterious effect on union density in countries with weak labor institutions, they contend that labor unions have grown in countries where collective bargaining, corporatism, and social welfare are well institutionalized.

These arguments support my analysis of why French, Italian, and Spanish unions have organized immigrants in distinct ways, which in turn shape their immigration policy preferences. Although interviews with labor leaders in all three countries revealed that they are concerned about the effects of globalization on union membership, in Italy, which has much higher overall unionization rates, unions have responded to immigrant workers differently from the French and Spanish unions.

The Italian unionization rates have held steady at about 33 percent of the workforce. Relative to other industrialized countries' unionization rates, Italy moved from eleventh place in 1970 to ninth in 1989. On the other hand, Spain and France have the lowest unionization rates in Europe, at about 10 percent of the workforce (Lange and Scruggs 1998, 7). The Spanish and French unions have found it difficult to attract immigrant members, and the proportion of the immigrant workforce affiliated with a union is even lower than among native workers. In Italy, on the other hand, 67 percent of legally employed immigrants are affiliated with a union. This is largely because of the organizing efforts of the Italian unions and the unique model of parallel immigrant membership organizations set up by the Confederazione Italiana Sindicati Lavoratori (CISL) and the Unione Italiana de Lavoro (UIL). These immigrant membership organizations are sponsored by the unions and are open to illegal and unemployed immigrants. Italian labor leaders view parallel immigrant organizations as a stepping stone for immigrant membership in the union. As a result, Italian labor leaders have been active proponents of the sponsored immigration quota, in which nongovernmental organizations that promise to provide housing and employment can bring immigrants to Italy. In contrast, French labor leaders are opposed to quotas because quotas select immigrant workers from one country or skill level over another, which is seen as inegalitarian. In Spain, most labor leaders support quotas, but as a means to legalize immigration flows, not to increase union membership.

How do these findings contribute to the convergence/divergence debate? My analysis of how labor leaders and employers form their immigration policy preferences and influence the policy-making process shows that a cursory examination of globalization and its effects misses distinctions in preference formation and policy outputs that result from domestic factors. Globalization plays a role in shaping aggregate preferences and policies across countries, but domestic factors filter its effects. As a result, neither labor leaders' nor employers' immigration preferences are identical across countries.

Research Scope

This book examines labor union leaders' and employers' immigration policy preferences and their influence in the immigration policy-making process. Consequently, my concern is more with how policy-making is influenced by formal institutions and processes, such as unions, employers' associations, and government ministries, than with informal institutions, such as immigrant organizations and the experience of immigrant workers (though immigrant organizations are discussed in the context of their relationship with unions and the policy-making process). My findings are based on interviews with labor union leaders, employer representatives, and government officials, as well as on union literature and analysis of media reports.

Many of the union representatives I interviewed readily admit that their members are not united behind their union's stance on immigration. This is especially true in France, where the anti-immigrant National Front has infiltrated the rank and file in sectors such as transportation. To convince their membership that the best strategy is more open immigration policies, French, Italian, Spanish, and U.S. unions are initiating educational programs for the rank and file. Despite internal discord, union leaders believe that immigration reform will ultimately benefit both immigrant and native workers, and they continue to pursue their immigration policy agenda. For these reasons, I focus on the immigration policy preferences of labor union leaders rather than rank-and-file members. Similarly, my research on employers' immigration preferences is based on interviews with employer representatives from national, regional, and sectoral employers' associations, rather than on discussions with individual employers.

When I began this research in 1996, Spanish, Italian, and French unions had established their preferences for more open immigration policies and already were important actors in the policy-making process. These three cases establish the framework chapters that explain labor union leaders' and employers' immigration policy preferences, as well as analyze how these groups have influenced the policy-making process.

U.S. unions lagged behind their European counterparts in reassessing their position on immigration. Although several unions affiliated with the AFL-CIO had begun to advocate changes to U.S. immigration policy in the mid-1990s, this reform swell did not reach the national level of the organization until the late 1990s. In October 1999, several key unions in immigrant-dominated sectors brought a proposal for immigration reform to the AFL-CIO national convention. In 2000, the

AFL-CIO's Executive Council developed a statement on immigration reform and held a series of "immigration town hall" meetings across the United States

This recent change in the immigration stance of U.S. labor leaders presented me with an opportunity to test whether the variables I use to explain Spanish, Italian, and French policy preferences could be applied elsewhere. However, it also created a problem for the book's organization, since incorporating a full analysis of the change in American labor leaders' nascent immigration preferences and their limited influence on immigration policy was premature. Therefore, in a separate chapter on the U.S. case I apply my variables to it and offer some tentative conclusions about the potential for a coalition between American business and labor to shape immigration policy outcomes.

Why Compare Spain, Italy, France, and the United States?

The Spanish, Italian, French, and U.S. cases make for interesting comparisons along several dimensions. First, each country has a complex migration history. Spain was a labor exporter for more than five hundred years. Only in the mid-1980s did the number of return migrants begin to exceed the number of emigrants. Italy, like Spain, has a long history of emigration, and just from the 1950s to the early 1970s, more than seven million people left Italy. However, by the late 1970s, Italy was experiencing net inflows of migrants resulting from repatriation and immigration.

This experience helped Italian and Spanish unions to sympathize with immigrant workers and left them better prepared to handle relevant issues than most societal actors and government agencies. In the late 1980s and 1990s, Spanish and Italian unions became leading advocates for more moderate immigration policies and primary providers of immigrant services, such as language training and legal assistance.

Today, the total number of immigrants in Spain (1.3 percent of the population) and Italy (1.7 percent) remains small compared to the number in France (6.3 percent) and the United States (9.7 percent). It is important to reiterate, however, that substantial immigration began there only in the mid-1980s. According to the Spanish Ministry of

Labor and Social Affairs, Spain had a legal immigrant population of only 182,045 in 1980. By 1998, this number had more than tripled, to 659,599. Similarly, Italy had 450,227 legal immigrants in 1985. By the end of 1998, this number had nearly tripled, to 1,250,214 (Caritas di Roma 1999). Today, the immigrant population in these countries continues to grow as a result of both legal and illegal immigration.

France and the United States have much longer histories of immigration. But neither country has recent experience with large-scale emigration. In 1946, 1,743,619 immigrants lived in France, comprising 4 percent of the population. By 1975, this number had grown to 3,442,415, with immigrants making up 6.5 percent of the population. Although the French government temporarily suspended new employment-based immigration in 1974, about 200,000 people per year continued to enter the country as a result of family reunification and political asylum. By 1982, France had an immigrant population of 3,714,200, with immigrants comprising 6.8 percent of the population (INSEE 1996). Today the French government accepts, on average, 100,000 new immigrants each year, primarily on the basis of family reunification and asylum.

Because of the country's long history of immigration, the French case allows for analysis of the changing preferences of employers and labor union leaders. In the 1960s, the CNPF actively promoted open immigration policies. But today the organization does not take a public stance on immigration. Like the Spanish and Italian national employers' organizations, it prefers to take a back seat on the issue.

Unlike Spain, Italy, and France, the United States is a "nation of immigrants" that has experienced continuous waves of immigration throughout its history. Since the early 1800s, it has admitted over 65 million immigrants. And in the 1990s, permanent immigration to the United States reached historic highs not seen since the early 1900s. From 1990 to 1998, 7,605,068 permanent immigrants were admitted, compared to 7,338,062 in the 1980s and 4,493,314 in the 1970s. Also, an all-time high of 30.1 million nonimmigrant visas (students, tourists, temporary workers, and diplomats) were issued in 1998. In addition to permanent and temporary immigration, in 1996 the Immigration and Naturalization Service (INS) estimated the undocumented immigrant population to be about 5 million and growing at a rate of 275,000 per year (U.S. Department of Justice 2000). Because of the U.S. immigration experience, immigration policy is debated in terms fundamentally different from those current in Spain, Italy, and France. In the United States, often what is up for debate is the number of available visas in a given year, not whether the country should continue to admit immigrants. In contrast, it is only in the last few years that many European policy-makers have completely discarded the idea of a zero-immigration policy.

The second interesting dimension of comparison among Spain, Italy, France, and the United States relates to the size of their underground economies. In Spain and Italy, the underground economy is pervasive—accounting for about 20 to 25 percent of gross domestic product (GDP). In Italy, illegal immigrants make up 14 percent of the 4,974,900 workers without an employment contract. The vast majority of these more than 700,000 illegal immigrants work in the service sector, where immigrants comprise 84 percent of the irregular workforce (Caritas di Roma 1997, 273). Italian and Spanish labor leaders want to reduce the size of the underground economy and believe legalizing illegal immigrants is a means to achieving this goal. On the other hand, in France the underground economy represents less than 15 percent of GDP, while illegal immigrants constitute only 2.5 percent of the total underground employment (author interview, Claude Valentine Marie, Head of Research, Interministerial Commission for the Fight Against Clandestine Work, Paris, September 15, 1997). Likewise, in the United States, the underground economy makes up less than 10 percent of GDP (Schneider and Enste 2000). Thus, for French and U.S. labor leaders, reducing the size of the underground economy is not a top priority.

A third interesting area of comparison concerns how unions in these four countries approach immigrant workers and how these unions have gained influence in the immigration policy-making process. The Spanish and French unions, with the lowest membership density in Europe at less than 10 percent of the workforce, have not emphasized immigrant membership. Nevertheless, Spanish unions are strengthened politically and organizationally through their national networks of social service centers for immigrants. Similarly, in the 1970s, the French unions harnessed immigrant worker militancy to gain political clout and win workplace rights for immigrants. In the United States, unionization rates have been steadily declining since the 1950s and today are a meager 15 percent of the workforce. Until recently, the leadership of the AFL-CIO was complacent about this loss of membership (Nissen 1999, 11). In the mid-1990s, however, a newly elected leadership team placed top priority on union organizing efforts as a means to gain more political clout. Many affiliated unions of the AFL-CIO in immigrant-dominated sectors have targeted unorganized immigrant workers in organizing drives. Italy, where unionization rates are more than 30 percent, represents a contrast to Spain, France, and the United States. Italian unions have focused on organizing immigrants in addition to providing immigrant services and advocating for more moderate immigration policies.

Plan of the Book

In Chapter 2, I develop a scale to measure the openness–restrictiveness of specific indices of immigration policy, namely legalization, quotas, family reunification, and work permits. These indices were chosen because they deal with aspects of labor immigration, as opposed to policies that address asylum or the social and political integration of immigrants already present in their host country. Indices are defined as very restrictive, restrictive, moderately open, open, or very open, then scored on a five-point scale, with one being very restrictive and five being very open. This scale is used to demonstrate how Spanish, Italian, and French immigration policies have become more open in the 1990s.

In Chapters 3 and 4, I turn to the immigration policy preferences of Spanish, Italian, and French labor leaders and employers. Several variables are offered in Chapter 3 to explain change in labor union leaders' preferences. Ideology is a partial, but, I argue, not a sufficient explanation. A more complete explanation can be found by examining some specific effects of globalization: since labor leaders believe that globalization challenges the state's capacity to control immigration, threatens union organization, and encourages the growth of the underground economy, they are taking a practical position by supporting moderate immigration policies.

Spanish, Italian, and French employers, on the other hand, often have ambiguous and contradictory immigration policy preferences. The changes in the French situation, analyzed in Chapter 4, illustrate how globalization, filtered through domestic institutions, has produced divergent preferences among employers of different sizes, regions, and sectors, though within the same country.

Chapter 5 focuses on the immigration policy-making processes in Spain, Italy, and France. The role of labor leaders is emphasized because national employers' associations have not taken an active position on immigration. Labor leaders have used a variety of tactics to shape immigration policy, such as formal contacts with government officials, informal contacts, and protest. Several factors help explain patterns of moderation in immigration policy, such as changes in government, institutional control over the policy-making process, and economic performance. However, the ascendancy of labor unions in the policy-making process, especially in Spain and Italy, is crucial to the recent moderation of immigration policy.

In Chapter 6, I discuss how the 1997 Amsterdam Treaty has broadened authority for immigration policy, beyond the exclusive domain of European Union member states, to Community institutions. This expansion of authority means that unions and employers must widen their scope of influence to the regional level.

In Chapter 7, I return to how labor leaders and employers form their immigration policy preferences by reflecting on recent changes in the United States. The changing preferences of American labor leaders can be explained with variables similar to those that account for change in European labor leaders' preferences. On the other hand, U.S. employers, who are openly pro-immigration, offer an interesting contrast with their more ambivalent European counterparts. Because of recent changes in the AFL-CIO's immigration stance, U.S. business and labor leaders have found some common ground on immigration, making for a politically powerful, cross-party alliance to lobby for reform.

2

Are Spain, Italy, and France Moving toward More Open Immigration Policies?

In the 1970s and 1980s, global economic restructuring and restrictive immigration policies helped create a growing population of economically, socially, and legally precarious immigrant workers in most industrialized countries. However, restrictive immigration policies often fail to control immigration completely in the face of powerful push factors, such as overpopulation, unemployment, and poverty in developing countries. Consequently, receiving states may boost illegal immigration by restricting legal, employment-based immigration. With little opportunity to migrate legally, many people take advantage of clandestine immigration networks and employment opportunities in the underground economy.

Immigration policies that promote irregularity and precarious employment in the underground economy have marginalized many immigrants. In turn, this marginalization has stimulated a reaction from the left, especially labor union leaders.

Many union leaders are demanding less restrictive policies to promote the stability of immigrant workers. These policies include long-term work and residency permits, permanent residency status, and amnesties for undocumented immigrants. For example, in the mid-1990s the French Confédération Générale du Travail (CGT) and Confédération Française Démocratique du Travail (CFDT) rallied on behalf of *sans-papiers* (undocumented immigrants) who were trapped in a maze of regulations created by the restrictive Pasqua Laws. Similarly, Spanish labor unions successfully lobbied for an increase in the 1997 immigration quota. And Italian labor unions asked for, and got, an amnesty in the 1994 Dini Decree.

Employers operating in the underground economy benefit from restrictive immigration policies that institutionalize irregularity. But most employers operating in the legal economy say they would prefer more open immigration policies that guarantee a legal and legitimate immigrant labor force willing to do the work that native workers shun.

Immigration policies have evolved from highly restrictive measures in the 1980s to more open ones in the 1990s. Important aspects of Spanish, Italian, and French immigration policies have been changed to promote legal immigration over illegal. But at the same time, these governments have tried to reduce clandestine immigration by tightening border controls.

Measuring Changes in Immigration Policy: Indices of Labor Migration

Because my focus is on the labor market aspects of immigration policy, I do not consider policies that deal with asylum or the social and political rights of legally resident immigrants. Instead, I focus on four aspects of immigration policy that deal specifically with labor migration: immigration quotas, work and residency permits, family reunification, and legalization. The crucial aspect of these policies is whether they promote illegal immigration and "institutionalized irregularity" (Calavita 1997) for immigrants by restricting immigration, or seek to advance legal immigration and immigrants' economic stability. For example, Spain's first immigration law of 1985 limited legal immigration to a few cases of asylum and family reunification for Americans and Europeans. As a result, North African immigrants had no choice but to immigrate illegally and enter the underground economy once they arrived in Spain. Reforms of the 1985 law helped to stabilize the situation of immigrants in Spain through extended work permits and two legalization procedures, and opened an avenue for legal immigration through employment-based quotas and more expansive family reunification policies.

In defining policies in each of these areas, I use the terms "very restrictive" (VR), "restrictive" (R), "moderately open" (MO), "open" (O) and "very open" (VO). Each definition is assigned a number from one to five, with one being the most restrictive and five being the most open.[1]

Quotas: Guaranteeing a Legal Avenue for Immigration

Quotas are often perceived as a means to limit, or restrict, immigration. However, I define employment-based quotas as an avenue for legal immigration. Without employment-based quotas, legal immigration is limited to family reunification or political asylum, so those who migrate for economic reasons must resort to illegal means. Ideally, quotas can help receiving states meet their labor market needs through legal immigration. Without quotas, employers may resort to hiring illegal immigrants. According to the objectives of the Spanish immigration reform of 1991, quotas should serve two purposes. First, they should channel legal immigration flows to sectors of the economy with a shortage of native labor. Second, they should help reduce illegal labor migration by providing an avenue for legal entry. Italy, like Spain, recently established a quota policy that seeks to channel legal immigration flows.

The French situation is more complex because the notion of quotas as a means to select and channel immigrant workers was rejected in the 1945 laws that laid down the basic outlines of France's immigration policy (Cornelius, Martin, and Hollifield 1994, 148). During the period of rapid economic growth from 1945 to 1974, immigration was a crucial aspect of France's industrial policy and technically was under the control of the National Immigration Office. However, official immigration targets became unnecessary as a result of immigration from France's former colony of Algeria and unofficial employer recruiting. Since the

---

[1] My scale measures the openness of specific policies. It does not necessarily measure the effectiveness of these policies in regulating immigration flows.

suspension of employment-based immigration in 1974, around 20,000 immigrants have been admitted each year for employment purposes. In 1993, the "quota policy" fell into disuse under the leadership of Interior Minister Charles Pasqua (author interview, Marie Thérèse Join Lambert, Inspector General, Department of Social Affairs, Paris, September 22, 1997). However, the 1998 immigration law calls for controlled immigration based on the need for skilled labor. Hence, France does not have an implicit quota policy like those of Spain and Italy. Nevertheless, I assign France a value for "quota policy" based on estimated annual employment-based immigration.

In Spain and Italy, quotas are set annually according to labor market needs, which are determined by the Ministry of Labor with input from employers, unions, and other relevant government ministries. Although the process of setting quotas should be formulaic, it often becomes political, with employers, labor unions, and ministries lobbying for changes in the initial quota.

I define the nature of quota policies as follows:

- VR = No legal avenue for employment-related immigration, or quota equals zero.
- R = Highly selective and limited quotas for an exclusive category of workers.
- MO = Annual quotas set according to labor market needs for all categories of workers. Quotas often determined according to bilateral agreements with sending countries.
- O = Variable, annual quotas set according to labor market needs for all categories of worker. Generally open to immigrants from all countries.
- VO = No quota ceilings set. In other words, unlimited immigration.

Work and Residency Permits: Assuring Greater Employment Stability

Work and residency permits are often tied to a quota policy as a means to regulate immigrants' length of stay, location, and residency status. Work and residency permits may be issued together by one government agency, typically the local police representing the Ministry of the Interior. Alternatively, the immigrant may have to petition the local police for a residency permit and the local representative of the Ministry of Labor for a work permit. Therefore, how permits are issued and by whom indicates the degree of policy openness. The more complex the application process, and the more discretion given to local officials, the more likely immigrants will fall into periods of illegality. In addition, the length of the initial permit is an important measure of openness, as well as the length of renewals and whether a renewal is contingent on having a job and housing. Finally, whether limited work and residency permits lead to permanent residency is another measure of openness.

Work and residency permits are categorized as follows:

- VR = No system of work and residency permits.
- R = Discretion over work and residency permits is delegated to the local police. Initial permit is granted for one year or less, and immigrant is tied to a specific employer. Renewals are contingent on continued employment with original employer and housing. No permanent residency.
- MO = Granting of work and residency permits is delegated to the local police and/or local labor officials. Initial permits are granted for at least one year, and employment may be in any sector. Renewals are granted for at least two years, contingent on sufficient income and housing. Permanent residency status can be obtained after five to six years of temporary status.
- O = Granting of work and residency permits is handled by one local government agency with strict guidelines for granting permits that leave little discretion to local authorities. Initial permits are granted for five-year period; after five years immigrant can petition for permanent residency.
- VO = Permanent residency status granted immediately.

Family Reunification: Improving the Stability of Immigrant Workers

Although family reunification is usually thought of as a social aspect of immigration policy, it is important for labor immigration for two reasons. First, family reunification helps stabilize the situation of the immigrant worker whose spouse and children are either abroad or have immigrated illegally. Second, family reunification contributes to the expansion of the labor market by adding spouses and eventually children. To measure the openness of family reunification policies, I consider whether family members can obtain a work permit; the time, income, and housing requirements for bringing family members into the receiving country; and which family members are included. Family reunification is defined as follows:

- VR = No family reunification.
- R = Spouses and minor children only. No work permits granted to family members. Immigrant must wait at least two years before he/she can bring family members and must show evidence of sufficient income and housing.
- MO = Spouses and minor children only. Spouse may obtain a work permit. Immigrant can bring family after one year or with proof of adequate income and housing.
- O = Unlimited and immediate family reunification for spouses, minor children, and parents. Quota system for married children and siblings set annually. Family members may obtain work permits. No income or housing requirement.
- VO = No restrictions on family reunification.

Legalization: Bringing Illegal Immigrants to the Surface

Legalization, also called amnesty or regularization, is the process of bringing illegal immigrants to light by granting them temporary legal status. Because it recognizes and regularizes clandestine populations, legalization is by its nature an open immigration policy. According to a French immigration expert, "amnesties typically happen when the government feels too many people are living outside the law" (author interview, Claude Valentine Marie, Head of Research, Interministerial Commission for the Fight Against Clandestine Work, Paris, September 15, 1997). In other words, legalization represents at least a temporary correction for policies that forced immigrants into illegal status.

Nevertheless, the specific parameters of an amnesty can make it more or less open. For example, an amnesty may be administered on a case-by-case basis or more generally, given certain criteria such as employment status and arrival date. Whether employers are also granted amnesty for employing illegal immigrants is an important criterion, since most illegal immigrants employed in the underground economy cannot show proof of employment unless their employer is also willing to come forward. In addition, legalization may be available only to "undocumented" immigrants who entered the country legally and whose permits have expired, or also to immigrants who entered the country illegally.

- VR = No legalization procedure.
- R = No legalization procedure.
- MO = Limited legalization on a case-by-case basis.
- O = Legalization for undocumented immigrants who at one time had legal status and can prove employment and housing.
- VO = General amnesty for illegal immigrants who arrived before a specific date and for employers who hired illegal immigrants.

Spanish Immigration Law: Correcting for Past Mistakes

Stimulated by a growing legal and illegal immigrant population and pending European Community membership, the Spanish government addressed immigration policy for the first time in 1985. The 1985 Ley Orgánica sobre Derechos y Libertades de los Extranjeros en España (Organic Law on the Rights and Freedoms of Aliens in Spain, or LOE) reaffirmed that immigrants held social, economic, and some political rights that had been guaranteed by the Spanish Constitution of 1978.[2] According to its preamble, the LOE had the dual purpose of guaranteeing immigrants' rights and controlling illegal immigration. However, because the text of the law was vague and imprecise concerning how Spain should control immigration, much subsequent policy was made by administrative decree, and its elaboration delegated to regional and provincial authorities.

---

[2] In 1985, the European Commission insisted in a memo to the European Council and Parliament on the need to harmonize immigration policy. The LOE became effective on July 1, 1985, just days after Spain signed the treaty for entry into the EC.

Two reforms of the 1985 law occurred in 1991 and 1996, and in 1999 a new organic law was passed. Because the original LOE failed to establish the administrative capacity necessary to regulate immigration, and many of its provisions were poorly devised, illegal entries resulted, legal immigrants were unable to renew their permits, and the illegal immigrant population in Spain expanded. The 1991 reform sought to correct for some of these deficiencies by clarifying Spain's quota policy and legalizing illegal immigrants. The 1991 reform also tried to better institutionalize the policy-making process through the creation of government offices dedicated to immigration. The 1996 reform further moderated Spanish immigration policy by increasing the length of work and residency permits, opening another amnesty, and easing restrictions on family reunification. The 1999 law replaces the 1985 LOE. The new organic law seeks to improve the social and economic integration of legal immigrants and open more doors for legal immigration including an ongoing legalization mechanism for illegal immigrants who have resided continuously in Spain for five years. Before discussing these reforms, I examine how the 1985 law restricted immigration to Spain and placed many immigrants in a precarious legal and employment situation.

The 1985 law established the principle of quotas tied to work permits. Quotas were to be determined annually by evaluating labor market needs that cannot be met by Spanish workers. Official annual quotas were not set until 1993, however, and quotas were not used effectively to channel legal immigration flows. Often the quota policy was used to legalize undocumented immigrants already in Spain. Because private employers were not required by law to post vacancies with the government, it was impossible to accurately determine the need for immigrant labor. So in practice, the process of determining quotas was administrative, and at times political. Essentially, the Ministry of Labor and Ministry of the Interior established the numbers with input from labor unions, employers' organizations, the Ministry of Agriculture, and provincial governments.

Several different classes of work permits were created by the LOE, and were categorized according to self-employment, contract employment, and length of stay. For contract employment, there were three types of permits. Permit A was for nine months. It could not be renewed, and it was limited to a specific employer. Permit B was for one year. It could be renewed for two years, but renewal depended on continued employment with the original employer. Permit C was a three-year permit enabling employment in any region or sector, and was renewable for two years. For self-employment there were two types of work permits. Permit D was for one year. It could be renewed for two years and was limited to a predetermined geographic location. Permit E was for three years, enabled employment in any region or sector, and was renewable for two years. Finally, permit F was for seasonal immigrant workers. Most permits granted to non-EU immigrants were for one year or less (see Figure 3), and were sector-and location-specific.[3]

Of 121,663 work permits issued by the Ministry of Labor in 1996, 70,828 (58%) were in services, 24,031 (20%) were in agriculture, and 11,766 (10%) were in construction. By limiting most permits to one year and to jobs that Spanish workers do not want, the Spanish government institutionalized precarious employment for the majority of immigrant workers. In addition, the administrative difficulties and delays in renewing work permits, which could last up to eight months, meant that many immigrants fell into periods of illegality (Calavita 1997, 28).

The 1985 law also provided for sanctions against employers who hired illegal immigrants. Employer sanctions were first implemented in 1988, but they did not deter most employers from illegal hiring. The sanctions were ineffective for three reasons. First, employers violating the law could be fined, but no criminal sanctions were levied against them. Second, inspections carried out by the Ministry of Labor included all aspects of labor violations, including health and safety violations, nonpayment of social security and nonadherence to collective bargaining agreements. Typically only those employers who committed the most extreme abuses of other labor standards were penalized for hiring illegal immigrants. Finally, neither illegal immigrant workers nor labor unions reported employer violations because the illegal immigrant worker did not enjoy immunity from expulsion.

Under the LOE, non-EC immigrants were required to have visas, and those who intended to stay in Spain longer than ninety days needed

---

[3] In 1991, work permits granted include those legalized in the 1991 amnesty, which contributed to the large increase in work permits between 1990 and 1991.

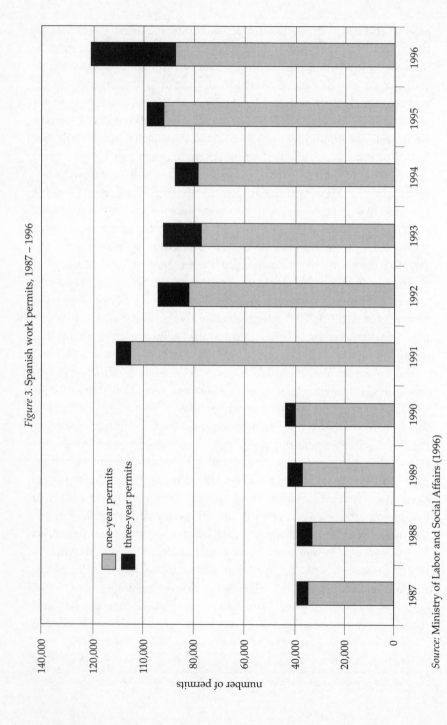

Figure 3. Spanish work permits, 1987 – 1996

one-year permits

three-year permits

number of permits

140,000

120,000

110,000

80,000

60,000

40,000

20,000

0

1987 1988 1989 1990 1991 1992 1993 1994 1995 1996

Source: Ministry of Labor and Social Affairs (1996)

work and residency permits. Therefore, the LOE inadvertently catego-rized most non-EC foreigners already living in Spain as illegal immi-grants. To remedy this problem, immigrants who had partial documen-tation and resided in Spain prior to 1985 were given the opportunity to apply for amnesty. However, only 44,000 undocumented immigrants applied. Of these, only 23,000 received legal status. The small number of applications was due in part to a lack of administrative infrastruc-ture to inform immigrants and process their applications, and to the fear of deportation that gripped most undocumented immigrants.

Even after immigrants were regularized, it was extremely difficult for them to maintain legal status because renewing a work permit re-quired proof that the original conditions of employment still existed. Some immigrants did not qualify for renewals because the work con-tracts on which their regularizations were based ended, or contracts were never fulfilled by employers. Of those regularized in 1985, only one-third were still legal after three years (Pumares 1996, 59).

Interestingly, the LOE made no mention of family reunification for immigrants. This official ambiguity was rectified by several adminis-trative decrees that detailed how immigrants seeking family reunifica-tion would receive preferential treatment for visas and work and resi-dency permits. In essence, the family member residing in Spain had to be well established, with at least three years' residency, and had to have the economic means to support the applicant. Exceptions to this restric-tive policy were made for immigrants from the EC, Latin America, Canada, the United States, Australia, Equatorial Guinea, Israel, Japan, and New Zealand. Two of the largest immigrant groups, those from the Maghreb and the Philippines, were excluded from the list. From 1992 to 1994, a ban was placed on issuing visas for family reunification. As a result, immigration under the auspices of family reunification was vir-tually impossible for most third-world immigrants until the reform of 1996 (Calavita 1997, 26).

The LOE largely failed to regulate legal immigration flows. Instead, its lack of clarity and its restrictiveness heightened immigrant insecu-rity and forced many immigrants into clandestine status. From 1986 to 1990, the weaknesses of the 1985 law became apparent from the grow-ing illegal immigrant population, the poor implementation of em-ployer sanctions, and the failure to implement the quota policy. In response, labor unions and many nongovernmental organizations began advocating a reform of the work permit system and a new amnesty. Major administrative reforms in 1991 and 1996 helped to clarify and open Spanish immigration policy.

In 1990, the Spanish parliament proposed to reform the 1985 law. The main objectives of this reform were to better channel immigration flows and better integrate immigrants into Spanish society. Channeling immigration flows did not mean closing Spain's doors to new immigration, but instead developing an immigration policy to direct flows according to the needs of the Spanish economy, fight against illegal immigration, and promote international cooperation.

The following aims were officially established by parliament in 1991:

- Develop and implement a quota system to organize immigration flows according to labor market needs and Spain's capacity to absorb immigrants.
- Modernize frontier controls.
- Complete the regularization process from 1985. In 1991 and 1992, 108,321 undocumented immigrants were regularized who could verify that they had been in Spain before May 15, 1991, had a work contract or were self-employed in a legitimate enterprise, or had a previously valid residence and work permit.
- Fight against the clandestine employment of foreign workers.
- Develop programs to promote the social integration of immigrants. Create an interministerial commission to coordinate policy among the Ministries of Labor, Interior, Justice, and Exterior.
- Help countries of emigration develop socially and economically, especially those in the Maghreb. Advance the integration of Spain into a Europe without frontiers by adhering to intergovernmental agreements such as Schengen (1985), which eliminates internal border controls among a subset of European Union member states.

These guiding principles for immigration reform were the impetus for several changes in administrative structures and procedures, including the creation of several government agencies focused on immigration and the establishment of a working quota policy. A central administrative body, the Interministerial Committee on Aliens, was created to coordinate the activities of the Ministries of Labor, Interior, and Exterior concerning work and residency permits and quotas. Offices for processing work and residency permit applications were established in several provinces. Within the Ministry of Labor and Social Affairs, a directorate was created to address migration flows, and another to work on programs for integrating immigrants into Spain. Within the Ministry of the Interior, a directorate was also created to be responsible for aliens. Finally, in 1995, the Foro para la Integración de los Inmigrantes (Forum for the Integration of Immigrants, FORO) was created so that government officials, labor unions, employers, nongovernmental organizations, and immigrant associations would have the opportunity to discuss immigration issues.

Despite its focus on improving administrative structures and helping integrate immigrants into Spanish society, the 1991 reform did not change the precarious situation of most immigrants who held short-term work permits. A second reform of the 1985 LOE, passed in February 1996, amended the system of work and residency permits with a one-year permit, which could lead to a two-year permit, followed by a three-year permit. If immigrants could prove uninterrupted legal status in Spain for six years, they became eligible for permanent residency. But although the creation of permanent residency status was a step toward greater moderation of Spanish immigration policy, the conditions for obtaining permanent residency were difficult to fulfill given the cumbersome renewal process during which immigrants often experienced periods of illegality.

The 1996 reform eased restrictions on family reunification and made it possible for a spouse to obtain a work permit. Spouses, minor children, and relatives who could prove economic dependence on the family member living in Spain became eligible for family reunification. In addition, previously legal immigrants whose work or residency permits had expired were given a four-month period to apply for amnesty. In 1996, 25,388 undocumented immigrants applied for amnesty (Ministry of Labor and Social Affairs 1996, 264).

Although the 1991 and 1996 reforms were important in loosening many of Spain's restrictive immigration regulations, the goal of immigration reformers was a new organic law that would replace the 1985 LOE. On December 22, 1999, after eighteen months of negotiations among Spain's political parties, parliament approved the Ley Orgánic sobre Derechos y Libertades de los Extranjeros en España y su Integración Social. The legislation called for:

- a continuous legalization mechanism for undocumented immigrants who could prove residency in Spain for at least two years;
- one-time amnesty for illegal immigrants arriving in Spain prior to July 1999;
- the right to family reunification for spouses, minor children, and dependent parents and grandparents;
- renewal of work permits for unemployed immigrants who at one time paid taxes and were eligible for unemployment benefits;
- the right to join a union and strike for legal and illegal immigrants.

The 1999 LOE passed by a slim majority in parliament. It was opposed by the conservative Partido Popular, which controlled the government but did not have enough votes to block the legislation. Many conservatives believed that the legislation would open the door to more illegal immigration because of new rights guaranteed to illegal immigrants and the continuous legalization mechanism. According to a representative of the Partido Popular, "Spain should be more prudent because it is a country on the frontier of the European Union" (Aizpeolea 1999).

In elections held in spring 2000, the Partido Popular won an absolute majority and promised to amend the 1999 LOE. On August 4, 2000, the Council of Ministers approved several government-sponsored reforms, such as increasing the waiting period for legalization from two to five years, and annulling new rights guaranteed to illegal immigrants, such as the right to strike and join a union.

In sum, the history of Spanish immigration policy shows an evolution from the restrictive LOE of 1985, to the moderating reforms of 1991 and 1996, and ultimately a new organic law in 1999. The purpose of the 1991 and 1996 reforms were to correct for the deficiencies of the 1985 LOE and promote legal immigration over clandestine immigration by:

- extending work permits, regularizing illegal immigrants, and expanding access to family reunification;

- permitting some legal immigration through employment-based quotas and family reunification;
- tightening administrative organization to better control the system of granting and renewing work permits and deporting illegal immigrants.

The 1999 LOE focused less on policies regulating the entry of immigrants and more on the political, social, and economic integration of legal and illegal immigrants. Although many of the social and political rights guaranteed to illegal immigrants were overturned in 2000, the 1999 LOE still promotes legal immigration over illegal through its ongoing legalization mechanism and more generous family reunification guidelines.

Since the late 1980s, the policy-making process in Spain has become more open and democratic. In the 1980s, immigration policy was exclusively the domain of government ministries which faced external pressures from other European countries to restrict immigration. In the 1990s, the mobilization of labor unions, immigrant associations, and other nongovernmental agencies forced the government to consider domestic immigration concerns. As a result, the policy-making process has come to reflect external considerations, such as maintaining good foreign relations with North African countries and complying with European immigration agreements, as well as domestic concerns, such as Spain's labor market needs.

Spain's trend toward moderation can be measured using my scale in which one represents the most restrictive immigration policy and five the most open. See Figure 4.

Italy: Closing the Gap between the Law and Its Implementation

The official goals of Italian immigration policy are to restrict illegal immigration while regulating legal immigration flows. However, a wide gap exists between Italian law and how it is implemented. One reason that Italian immigration law has been implemented poorly is that in the underground economy, which makes up about 25 percent of gross domestic product, employers and illegal immigrants are mutu-

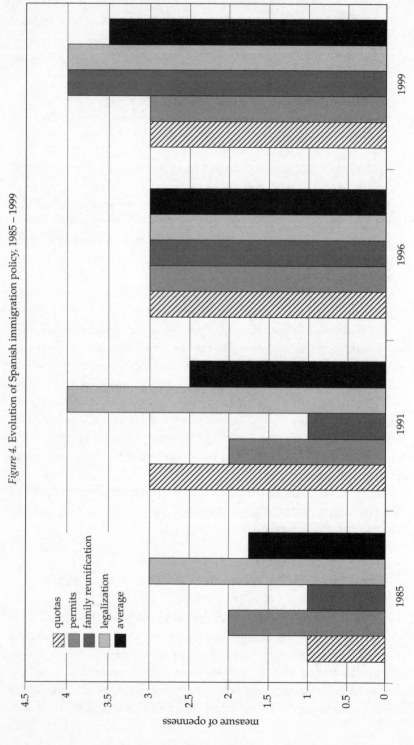

Figure 4. Evolution of Spanish immigration policy, 1985 – 1999

ally attracted to each other. Furthermore, because the black market is critical to Italian economic growth, the government is often unwilling to control it. In addition, frequent amnesties and Italy's ambiguous deportation procedures have ensured that illegal immigrants would not be expelled, and may have encouraged more illegal immigration. In sum, Italian immigration policy is often contradictory and executed inconsistently.

Italy, like Spain, first instituted a comprehensive immigration policy in the mid-1980s. Before the 1980s, Italian immigration policy was piecemeal and addressed only specific concerns such as how to apply for residency and work permits. The 1931 Law on Public Security, decreed by Mussolini as a security measure, which required foreigners to declare their presence to the police within three days of their entry into Italy, and other similar administrative acts meant to control the entry and stay of foreigners remained on the books until the 1980s (Christensen 1997, 467). These early administrative regulations made it almost impossible for an immigrant to enter Italy legally and they did little to control the flow of illegal immigrants.

To address the growing problem of illegal immigrants in the labor market, the Ministry of Labor decreed two limited amnesties in 1979 and 1982. The 1979 amnesty applied only to immigrants employed illegally as domestic workers and to those seeking domestic work. The 1982 legalization was slightly broader, offering amnesty to immigrants who were working for an Italian in any sector, and who had entered Italy before December 31, 1981. When the Ministry of Labor decreed the amnesty in 1982, Italy stopped granting work permits to non-EC citizens. The outcome of both amnesties was modest because the state did not announce them adequately, and because it lacked the resources to carry out legalization procedures. Nevertheless, these early steps established Italy's pattern of restricting legal flows, then regularizing illegal immigrants when faced with a growing population of illegal workers. In turn, this practice encouraged more illegal immigration.

By the mid-1980s, the number of illegal immigrants was estimated at one million. At the same time, the number of legal immigrants also increased. Between 1980 and 1985, the latter grew by more than 40 percent (Christensen 1997, 477). Rapid growth in the immigrant population, combined with media speculation that immigrants were responsible for several terrorist attacks in the early '80s, convinced the Italian parliament to address immigration policy for the first time.

The 1986 Law 943 had five main aspects. First, immigration was to be determined by Italian labor market needs. Second, an amnesty was used to address the situation of illegal employment. Third, government sanctions were introduced to punish employers who hired immigrants off-the-books, as well as traffickers of illegal immigrants. Fourth, to conform with international agreements, all legally resident alien workers and their families were declared to have the same rights as Italian workers. Fifth, family reunification was recognized for the first time for the children and spouses of legally resident aliens.

The 1986 law did little to ameliorate the problems of illegal immigration. The system of administrative decrees that controlled the entry and stay of immigrants remained in effect, and the linking of new entries to labor market demands gave the Ministry of Labor added authority to decree more restrictions on immigration. The amnesty failed to dramatically reduce the illegal immigrant population in Italy. Only 105,000 foreigners were legalized under the amnesty because of a lack of publicity and poor administrative coordination between the national and regional levels.

Although they were guaranteed the same rights as Italian workers under Law 943, immigrants were not eligible to renew their permits unless they were employed at the time they made the request. Therefore, although they could not be deported for losing their jobs, immigrants could still be forced to leave the country if they did not find new jobs before their permits expired.

Between 1986 and 1990, immigration to Italy continued to grow, and social groups concerned with the issue made the debate more public. In September 1989, the labor unions led a mass demonstration in Rome, reacting to the murder of a South African immigrant by a group of young Italians. European politics also added pressure to reform immigration law and curb illegal immigration, as these measures were a prerequisite for Italy joining the open-border Schengen group.

In September 1989, socialist Vice Prime Minister Claudio Martelli proposed new legislation that was meant to address the concerns of the unions and nongovernmental organizations and bring Italy in line with European conventions. Martelli advocated a "tolerant" law that recognized Italy's "duty to help the development of the South of the world and to welcome its population in Italy" (Christensen 1997, 482). But Martelli also asserted that Italy's immigration policy must be "aligned and coherent with the choices of other occidental nations" (La Repubblica 1990, as cited in Thranhardt 1992, 210).

Martelli's proposal faced opposition in parliament from the conservative minority, which favored more restrictive measures. Nevertheless, it was approved by 90 percent of the parliament on February 20, 1990, after some minor modifications were made to expand police power to deport immigrants for criminal reasons.

The Martelli Law sought to reduce the number of illegal immigrants in Italy and discourage new illegal immigration, while controlling legal flows. In pursuit of the former, it included an amnesty that tried to mitigate employer resistance by not fining employers or forcing them to pay back taxes when they reported illegal hires. The opportunity to regularize was opened to self-employed illegal immigrants as well as those doing contract work. However, to be eligible, self-employed illegal immigrants had to meet a minimum education requirement, and their country of origin had to have a reciprocal agreement offering employment to Italian citizens. Still, the Martelli amnesty was much more successful than previous amnesties because it was better publicized via radio and television and better funded and staffed thanks to the help of unions and voluntary associations. Nearly 250,000 formerly illegal immigrants were legalized.

Under the Martelli Law, a policy was established in which annual quotas were determined according to labor market needs by the Ministry of Foreign Affairs with input from other ministries, labor unions, and employers' organizations. However, according to a Ministry official, quotas have not been met because of administrative requirements on employers, such as the need to specify in advance immigrants employers want to hire (author interview, Francesco Lanata, Minister Plenipotentiary for Immigration and Asylum, Ministry of Foreign Affairs, December 9, 1997). To qualify for legal immigration under the quota policy, a potential immigrant first had to show he had a job in Italy with an employer who guaranteed lodging. Then the potential immigrant obtained a visa from an Italian consulate abroad. Finally, he applied for a work permit from a local office of the Ministry of Labor.

Under the Martelli Law, a permit could be renewed for a period twice as long as its initial duration, provided the immigrant could show an income at least equal to the state pension. However, the police retained a great deal of discretion in renewing permits. Police could refuse to grant or renew permits to aliens who made late requests, did not have current visas, or who were deemed dangers to the security of the state, public order, or health. When denied a permit, the immigrant received a written report explaining the reasons for denial and could file a grievance.

The Martelli Law expanded the kinds of crimes for which deportation was permitted, though it failed to resolve deportation problems when an immigrant violated entry rules. Illegal aliens often evaded deportation by failing to obey written warrants to leave the country.

The law's main strength was its ability to reduce the number of illegal immigrants through a broad amnesty for both illegal immigrants and employers. It failed to deal adequately with new immigration flows because of weaknesses in the quota policy and deportation procedures. Between 1991 and 1997, conservative governments capitalized on these weaknesses by making several decrees designed to restrict immigration, the most important being the Dini Decree. Under pressure from other EU member states to reduce illegal immigration, and from the right-wing Northern League party to restrict immigration, the center-right government of Lamberto Dini issued a decree that allowed swifter deportations. Immigrants could challenge the deportation order by returning to Italy at their own expense.

The original decree of November 1995 was amended by parliament to include an amnesty and quota for non-EU seasonal workers. The most restrictive aspects of the decree, namely the increased police powers to detain and expel illegal immigrants, were dropped. Finally, the amended Dini Decree, issued in December 1996, established more severe sanctions for the trafficking and employment of illegal aliens.

The amnesty program required that the immigrant have a job and that the alien's employer pay a fine equal to six months of the immigrant's wages to the state social security fund. Legal aliens could regularize their spouses and children if they had proof of sufficient income and housing. Unemployed illegal immigrants could also obtain legal status by enrolling in a government hiring program and by providing proof that they had been employed for at least four of the previous twelve months. To regularize their status, unemployed illegal immigrants had to pay a fine equal to four months' wages. Under the Dini Decree, 147,479 immigrants were regularized (Caritas di Roma 1997, 236).

Despite government efforts to reduce illegal immigration, the problem persisted and blocked Italy's full membership in the Schengen group until spring 1998. The deportation rules, which allowed undocumented immigrants in violation of administrative codes to remain free until their expulsion date, made police enforcement of deportations extremely difficult. Italy's large underground economy, which is condoned by most Italian business people and government officials, also encouraged illegal immigration. Legislation that has made legal immigration a cumbersome bureaucratic process encouraged many immigrants to come to Italy illegally and wait for an amnesty, which Italy became well known for offering—three times within ten years.

The continuing problems of illegal immigration and a desire to join other European countries in an open-border agreement were the stimuli for drafting new immigration legislation in 1997, which was passed in March 1998. This new law seeks to be comprehensive by balancing external control policies with an internal expansion of social, economic, and political rights for legal immigrants. At the same time, the law is a compromise between the left, which favors more open immigration policies, and the right, which wants to restrict immigration and strengthen controls. It also suggests, in a general sense, that responsibility for immigration controls and social services be decentralized to the local level. For example, the law stipulates that the police commissioner, who represents the Ministry of the Interior at the local level, gain more discretion over deciding the length of residency permits. And though it establishes a maximum two-year residency permit for new immigrants, which can be renewed for a maximum of four years, some discretion is left to the local police commissioner to grant permits for less than the maximum time period.

The law allows immigrants, after five years of legal residency, to request permanent residency by establishing proof of self-sufficiency and adequate housing. This represents the first time permanent residency has been introduced into Italian immigration law.

The law seeks to remedy the problem faced by police in expelling un-documented immigrants who were allowed to remain free until their expulsion date. Under Article 12, immigrants who enter Italy without proper documentation, but cannot be immediately expelled, are to be placed in detention centers until their expulsion date. Detained immigrants are given the right of defense and cannot be held for more than twenty days without legal action.

The proposed quota policy is an important and innovative part of the law because it ends the old system of immigration based on illegal entry and regularization. The quota policy sets up a four-pronged system:

- A quota for dependent (or contract) workers determined at the local level by provincial governments, employers, and labor unions based on labor market needs. Immigrants are recruited through bi-lateral agreements with sending states. Quotas can be changed during the year if labor market needs change.
- A quota for autonomous workers determined at the local level with admission through bilateral agreements with sending states.
- A quota for immigrants sponsored by a public or private body that will provide support for them. A firm, private individual, or public agency can sponsor immigrants.
- A small quota for immigrants originating from countries not covered by bilateral agreements with Italy and who do not have a sponsor.

The principle behind the bilateral agreements is that sending states are required to take back immigrants who enter Italy illegally, whether those immigrants originate from the sending state or have only passed through it. In return, Italy provides technical assistance in police training and in economic development to sending states.

Policy-makers avoided the amnesty issue in writing the 1998 law because the Italian government was reluctant to have another amnesty before Italy gained full membership in Schengen in spring 1998. However, according to the new law, immigrants who entered Italy illegally before March 1998 cannot be expelled. The undefined legal status of many of these immigrants has been remedied by two amnesties. In the fall of 1998, 38,000 work permits were granted to employed immigrants who arrived prior to March 1998. Approximately 280,000 illegal immigrants applied. The Ministry of the Interior promised those who met the requirements, but were not granted a permit in 1998, that they could stay in Italy and would become eligible for the 1999 quota. In February 1999, Italy offered a second amnesty in which 300,000 immigrants applied and 150,000 received legal status.

The inability of the government to attack the demand for illegal immigrant labor at its source—in the underground economy—has debilitated legislative efforts to control illegal immigration. In fact, some policies, such as Italy's well-known deportation procedures and restrictions on legal immigration, may have actually encouraged more illegal immigration and created a group of institutionally illegal immigrants.

The new legislation seeks to remedy some of these problems by changing deportation procedures, levying heavier fines on those who hire and traffic illegal immigrants, and opening Italy's doors to legal immigration through a more expansive quota policy. However, implementing these new policies may prove extremely difficult. Structural problems include the lack of deportation centers and police to monitor Italy's long coastline and huge underground economy. More important, the political will to enforce measures against employers who hire illegal immigrants continues to be weak. According to one labor union leader, "Employer sanctions were provided for in each law [1986, 1990 and 1998] but few sanctions were actually made because the government benefits from the black market. Work inspectors do not want to enforce sanctions, especially in the South where violations are most prevalent, because inspectors fear for their lives" (author interview, Angelo Masetti, National Representative for Migration, UIL, Rome, December 3, 1997).

Italy's immigration policy, like Spain's, has generally become more open with regard to quotas, permits, and legalization, while taking a firmer approach to illegal entries through the establishment of deportation centers. Also, the Italian immigration policy-making process has become more democratic with increasing input from labor unions, employers, immigrant associations, and members of parliament. According to my scale, I have assigned values to the four major Italian immigration laws since 1986; see Figure 5.

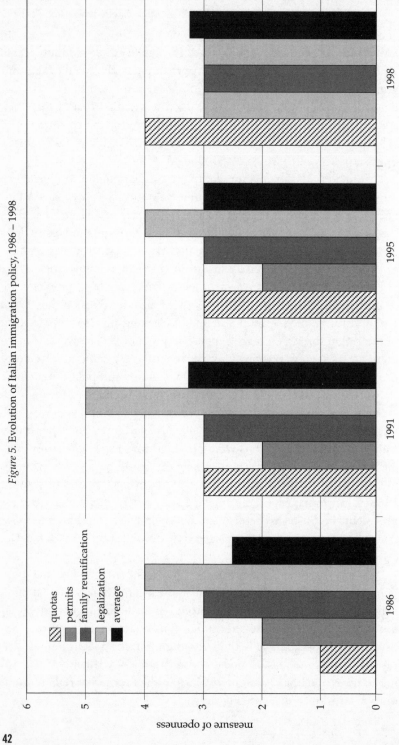

Figure 5. Evolution of Italian immigration policy, 1986 – 1998

France: From Moderation to Restriction and Back Again

In contrast to Spain and Italy, France has a much longer history of immigration. In the post–World War II period, the French state and private employers actively recruited immigrants, who they believed were essential to economic and demographic growth. This period of nearly laissez-faire immigration came to an abrupt end with the oil crisis of 1973. During the ensuing economic recession, France attempted to close its borders to new employment-based immigration, but for humanitarian reasons continued to admit large numbers of family members and asylum seekers. As temporary immigrants became permanent residents and eventually French citizens, policy-makers developed a complex institutional framework for immigration and focused increasingly on integration and assimilation policies.

The history of French immigration policy falls into two main parts, 1945–1974, and 1974 to the present. I have subdivided the post-1974 period by administration to discuss important changes that took place.

Laissez-Faire Immigration, 1945–1974

Until 1974, the main policy instrument that undergirded French immigration was the *ordonnance* of 1945. This administrative order required immigrants seeking employment in France to obtain a work and residency permit. It also established the National Immigration Office (ONI and later OMI) to control immigration flows.

Although the ONI had a legal monopoly over immigration, in practice it lost control over the recruitment process as private employers' demand for immigrant labor exceeded the ONI's capacity to deal with it. ONI's loss of control over immigration was reflected in the regularization, or legalization, rate, which jumped from 20 percent in 1950 to 50 percent in 1957, and by the late 1960s reached 90 percent (Hollifield 1998, 3). During this period, employers recruited in the sending countries, bringing undocumented workers to France. Once employed, a request for an adjustment of status, or *régularisation*, was filed with the ONI. To study the problem of private recruitment, an Interministerial Committee was convened in 1965, and this led to a reorganization of the ONI. And in 1966 the Department of Population and Migration was created to manage the immigration process from recruitment to naturalization. Despite these efforts to bring recruitment back under state control, however, many employers continued to recruit immigrant workers illegally and later legalize their status.

With its free market programs, the administration of President Georges Pompidou (1969–1974) did little to restrain employers from privately recruiting foreign labor. From 1968 to 1973, the average annual immigration rate was 341,000 and the legalization rate was 90 percent (Hollifield 1998, 3). During this time, slower economic growth and an increase in unemployment rates in the early 1970s, combined with increasing social tension over immigration, provided the stimuli for an administrative order to restrict it. The Marcellin-Fontanet administrative order of 1972 sought to end noncontractual immigration and link immigration more tightly to labor market needs. This administrative order established a complex bureaucratic system that required employers to find housing for immigrant workers and made it possible immediately to deport undocumented workers who were deemed a threat to the public order.

The Marcellin-Fontanet policies foreshadowed the economic crisis and suspension of employment-based immigration that would take place under the presidency of Valéry Giscard d'Estaing (1974–1981). The oil crisis of 1973 and the subsequent global economic recession brought a sudden end to almost thirty years of French economic growth, and a 1974 decree officially suspended the entry of new workers. When recruitment of immigrant workers was officially ended, foreigners made up 6.54 percent of the French population, and their number had almost doubled since the end of World War II, from 1,743,619 to 3,442,425 (INSEE 1997). It is important to note that immigration to France did not end after 1974. The number of immigrants continued to grow as a result of family reunification, asylum, and illegal immigration. By stopping worker immigration, the state indirectly encouraged foreign workers to stay and bring their families. After the ban on worker immigration in 1974, the percentage of family immigration increased as a portion of all immigration. Seasonal immigration and illegal immigration also became more prevalent. Nevertheless, 1974 marks a dramatic change in the nature of immigration and immigration policies.

French immigration policy up to 1974 can be described as laissez-faire, despite attempts by the state to set targets and control flows. The ONI was unable to keep up with employer demand for immigrant labor, which resulted in massive illegal immigration followed by legalization. Although the state set targets for immigration in its five-year economic plans, these targets were regularly outstripped.

Post-1974 Immigration Policies

French policy-making since 1974 has been characterized by two trends. First, the focus has shifted from immigration policies to immigrant policies, designed to help permanent immigrants assimilate into the French economy, culture, and society. For example, immigrants were granted important workplace rights in the early 1970s, such as the right to become shop stewards and the right to stand for elections to work committees (1975). Second, immigration policies have undulated according to left-right shifts in government. These changes in government provide the backdrop to the unfolding of French immigration policy.

Under the conservative governments of Prime Ministers Jacques Chirac and Raymond Barre (1974–1981) French immigration policy became increasingly restrictive. Dozens of decrees were proposed to limit immigration and family reunification and encourage the repatriation of immigrant workers and their families (Ireland 1994, 49). For instance, administrative decrees discouraged family reunification by restricting family members' access to the labor market. The Stoléru Decrees of 1979 imposed limits on the renewal of work and residency permits. And the Barre-Bonnet laws tightened rules against illegal immigrants and made deportation easier. However, most of these decrees were nullified by the Council of State, which, on many occasions, has protected immigrants from restrictive measures that would have violated their individual rights. For example, the 1974 ban on employment-based immigration also included a ban on family reunification, which was struck down by the French judiciary. Nevertheless, the Barre government set a restrictive tone that heightened the public debate on immigration. In the 1970s, restrictive immigration policies reduced annual immigration rates dramatically from 133,600 between 1968 and 1973 to 27,600 between 1974 and 1980 (Hollifield 1998, 3).

The restrictive policies of the Chirac and Barre governments left many immigrants on the margins of economic, social, and political life—particularly the numerous immigrants who had entered France illegally or whose legal status had expired. By the end of the 1980s, the number of illegal immigrants in France and their employment status were ambiguous and unknown.

In 1981, the election of President François Mitterrand and a socialist government turned the tide toward a moderation of immigration policy. During the elections, Mitterrand promised reforms that would improve the rights and security of immigrants in France, including greater protection against deportation without due process, eased restrictions on family reunification, a reform of the work and residency permit system, permanent residency status, and an amnesty.

Mitterrand's amnesty process began in 1981 and lasted into 1983. Illegal immigrants who had entered France before January 1981 were eligible for a temporary residency permit, valid for three months, which allowed them to complete an adjustment of status application. Illegal immigrants also had to show proof of employment, which was made easier because employers were also given amnesty for employing them. Over 150,000 applications for amnesty were filed, and 140,000 were approved (Marie 1994, 119).

The amnesty revealed that the economic climate of recession and high unemployment had a severe effect on immigrant workers who had been concentrated in the suffering car manufacturing and steel industries. In the 1970s and 1980s, large numbers of immigrants were laid off from these industries while newly arrived, illegal immigrants were virtually absent from them. Instead, immigrants were increasingly concentrated in small firms of fewer than ten employees (Marie 1994, 119). Because these firms had little or no union representation, the immigrants enjoyed little protection from employer abuses.

The goal of the work and residency permit reform was to help immigrants obtain the necessary permits and to ease their integration into French society by means of a ten-year residency and work permit.

The expansion of immigrants' rights and loosening of immigration policy under Mitterrand helped stimulate a right-wing reaction from Jean Marie Le Pen and his anti-immigrant National Front (FN) party. In the 1986 elections, Mitterrand lost the socialist majority in parliament. The new conservative government, under the leadership of Chirac, was under increasing pressure from the extreme right to restrict immigration. During the period of cohabitation between socialist President Mitterrand and conservative Prime Minister Chirac from 1986 to 1988, Chirac used much of Le Pen's anti-immigrant discourse to tie immigration to crime, drug addiction, and other social problems. The policies of Chirac and his interior minister, Charles Pasqua, rejected the idea of a multicultural France and emphasized the security aspects of immigration control. Pasqua unsuccessfully attempted to reform the Nationality Code of 1945, which would have denied automatic French citizenship to second-generation immigrants. Police powers were heightened, making it easier for police to deport immigrants believed to be a threat to public order. Finally, a quota system, which had been used to admit around 20,000 workers each year (30 percent of this 20,000 were managerial or technical workers), was discontinued (author interview, Marie Thérèse Join Lambert, Inspector General, Department of Social Affairs, Paris, September 22, 1997).

The second period of cohabitation during Mitterrand's presidency, 1992–1993, brought a further tightening of immigration policies. Under the leadership of Prime Minister Edouard Balladur and Interior Minister Pasqua, the traditional conservative parties attempted to wrest control over the anti-immigrant discourse from the right-wing National Front. The automatic right to French citizenship for second-generation immigrants born in France was taken away, so that second-generation immigrants had to apply for naturalization and take an official oath of allegiance to the French state. Police were given more power to detain and expel suspicious-looking immigrants who were deemed a threat to the public order, and immigration controls at the border were reinforced. Family reunification was restricted, requiring immigrants to wait two years, instead of one, to bring family members to France. An illegal immigrant could no longer become legalized automatically by marrying a French citizen. Finally, illegal immigrants were denied access to health care and social security. In addition to these policy changes, a new government office, the Office Central pour la Répression de l'Immigration Irrégulière et de l'Emploi sans Titres (Central office for the repression of irregular immigration and employment without contracts, OCRIEST), was established to monitor and control the employment of illegal immigrant workers. OCRIEST's mandate overlapped that of the existing Interministerial Mission for the Fight against Clandestine Work, which dealt with all forms of illegal work. In 1993, the Constitutional Council declared several of these provisions unconstitutional, including restrictions on family reunification and legalization by marriage. This set off a fierce national debate on immigration between the left and the right. In 1996, a newly elected conservative government led by President Chirac and Prime Minister Alain Juppé proposed legislation that closed any loopholes for illegal immigration left by the 1993 law and curbed immigration from Africa. The 1997 Debré law, named after Interior Minister Jean-Louis Debré, increased police powers to track immigrants in France and set strict income and housing requirements for granting visas. The Pasqua and Debré Laws and the politicization of the debate further marginalized immigrants by making them scapegoats for France's economic and social ills. Unemployment rates of 33 percent among immigrants, compared to approximately 12 percent total unemployment, and 50 percent among young immigrants are just one manifestation of institutionalized discrimination faced by immigrants (Direction de la Population et des Migrations 1995).

In the 1997 elections, the socialist party won control of parliament from the conservatives, ushering in a third period of cohabitation and a major alteration of French immigration policy. In his opening speech to the French parliament in June 1997, the new socialist prime minister, Lionel Jospin, argued that immigration is an economic, social, and human reality. Therefore, France must define a firm, dignified immigration policy without renouncing its values or compromising its social balance. Jospin laid out four components of such a policy: first, laws to welcome immigrants but combat illegal immigration and black labor markets; second, cooperation with sending states to help control immigration at its source; third, a comprehensive review of immigration and nationality law by an interministerial task force; and fourth, reviewing the situation of undocumented immigrants on a case-by-case basis. In 1997, 140,000 illegal immigrants applied for amnesty. As of September

1998, 76,000 immigrants had been granted legal status and 64,000 applicants had been rejected.

The interministerial task force review of immigration policy resulted in two reports that recommended 140 changes to existing immigration and nationality laws. The main author of the report, Patrick Weil, said that the goal was to find a consensus position between the center-left and center-right on immigration (author interview, September 22, 1997). The report took a market-oriented approach that recognized the inevitability of migration and the need for skilled labor immigration. At the same time, the report proposed reducing illegal immigration by attacking the source of demand in the labor market and better enforcing deportations. It also recommended reinforcing the rights of families by reducing the time requirement for reunification from two years to one, and by reducing the residency requirement for permanent status for immigrants marrying French citizens from two years to one. Income requirements on parents who wanted to bring their children to France, and the need for housing certification, were also eliminated.

With some minor modifications, the report was transformed into the Chevènement Law, named after the minister of the interior. According to Chevènement, France must be "very open on both welcoming immigrants and on bringing migratory flows under control. That is absolutely necessary and no party, on the right or left, disagrees with this" (Reuters 1997). The law, passed in the first quarter of 1998 by a narrow margin, rolls back some of the restrictive legislation passed in 1993 and 1997.

After the long period of open immigration from the end of World War II to 1974, French immigration policy has alternated between restriction and moderation. Under the latest legislation, France has taken a more moderate stance on employment-based immigration, family reunification, and legalization. According to my scale, I assign the values shown in Figure 6 to periods of French immigration policy since 1945.

Conclusion

Restrictive immigration policies create a situation of institutionalized precariousness for many immigrants, who find themselves caught in a bureaucratic tangle of regulations or immigrate illegally because no av-

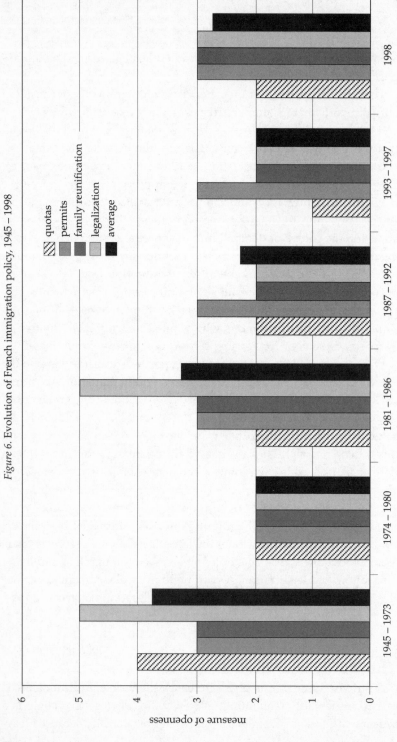

Figure 6. Evolution of French immigration policy, 1945 – 1998

enues are open for legal immigration. In the 1970s and 1980s, economic restructuring combined with restrictive immigration policies left many immigrants unemployed or underemployed in France, and marginalized immigrants in the underground economies of Spain and Italy. At the same time, globalization was facilitating migration and strengthening migration networks by making transportation and communication technology more accessible, which in turn weakened the states' ability to completely control immigration.

The effects of restrictive policies on immigrants created an intolerable situation for many labor unions, nongovernmental organizations, and immigrant associations. In the next chapter, I explore labor leaders' reaction to immigration restrictions imposed in the 1970s and 1980s.

This chapter has drawn an important lesson about the evolution of immigration policies, from restrictive measures in the 1970s and 1980s, which promoted illegal immigration and institutionalized irregularity for many immigrants, to more open policies in the 1990s. Moderation does not mean opening the gates to large numbers of new immigrants. In fact, administrative controls over deportations of illegal immigrants have increased. Instead, moderate policies are those that help secure legal avenues for immigration through family reunification and employment-based immigration, and promote the legal and economic stability of immigrants through legalizing illegal immigrants and extending work and residency permits.

3

Why Labor Union Leaders Prefer More Open
Immigration Policies

Despite legal guarantees of workplace equality between native and immigrant workers, such as equal pay for equal work, globalization and restrictive immigration policies have combined to relegate most immigrant workers to the margins of the labor market. Based on their ideological perspective that all workers should be equal regardless of their country of origin, most labor union leaders find such restrictive policies unacceptable. Yet, although this internationalist, working-class ideology helps explain why many labor leaders defend the rights of immigrant workers, ideology is not the whole story. A more complete explanation—one that addresses the variance in labor leaders' immigration preferences over time—must focus on changes in the global economy since the mid-1970s.

Although most labor leaders generally support moderate immigration policies, cross-nationally and among unions in the same country, they often have distinct policy preferences. For example, French labor leaders favor legalizing illegal immigrants only on humanitarian grounds, whereas Spanish and Italian leaders support legalization for economic reasons, since they believe legalization helps bring illegal immigrants out of the underground economy. These variations can be explained by domestic factors, such as the pervasiveness of the underground economy in Italy and Spain compared to France.

In the wake of increasing economic openness and competition, many labor union leaders have realized that the state can no longer control immigration completely (see Haus 1995). In Spain, Italy, and France, this attitude began to take hold only in the early 1980s. In fact, as recently as the mid-1970s, the leadership of the French Confédération Générale du Travail (CGT) and Force Ouvrière (FO) supported suspending labor immigration. They believed that a temporary ban on employment-based immigration was a feasible and necessary measure to get France through economic crisis. However, since the mid-1980s, labor leaders have increasingly doubted the efficacy of restrictive immigration policies.

Labor leaders have changed their views for three reasons. First, globalization challenges the ability of receiving states to control their borders by making communication and transportation technology more accessible to migrants and by opening economies to greater international trade and capital flows. These trends, in turn, accentuate demand for cheap labor in receiving states and increase the supply of unemployed labor in sending states.

Whether globalization has a direct, deleterious effect on union membership is uncertain because many domestic factors intervene between expanding global competition and union density (see Golden 1997; Lange and Scruggs 1998; Wallerstein 1989). Nevertheless, many labor union leaders believe that global competition erodes traditional work relations, and as a result diminishes sources of union membership. Hence, unions are experimenting with programs and institutions that appeal to new kinds of workers in unconventional work relations (see Ness 1998). Women, young people, and immigrants are examples of this new, often precarious workforce, in which workers are often employed part-time, on a temporary basis, or without a contract.

The second reason labor leaders have changed their immigration policy preferences centers around union organization. For instance, Spanish and Italian unions provide legal services to immigrants who wish to regularize their status, reunite with their families, and renew their work and residency permits. Because they provide these extensive services on the local level, unions have become important advocates for immigrants on the national level, where they lobby for more moderate immigration policies.

Third, secondary and underground economies are expanding as alternatives to the highly regulated formal economy. Because global economic competition from low-wage countries threatens the profitability of many labor-intensive firms, some employers, to improve their earnings, move production to the largely unregulated secondary and underground economies. In turn, this threatens wages, working conditions, and the power of labor unions to regulate the labor market.

Many labor leaders believe that by imposing restrictive immigration policies, the state encourages illegal immigration. Since most illegal immigrants work without a formal employment contract, many labor leaders link an increase in illegal immigration with the growth of the underground economy. Labor leaders, who fear that an expanding underground economy undercuts workers' wages and protections in the formal economy, want to bring the underground economy to the surface. They therefore prefer policies that promote legal immigration over illegal.

In this chapter, I discuss how ideology provides a foundation for many labor leaders' transnational perspectives, then explore how changes in the global economy interact with domestic factors to shape labor leaders' preferences for moderately open immigration policies.

Ideology: A Necessary but Insufficient Explanation

Before a phenomenon like migration, with thousands of people moving around the world in search of better living conditions, the distinction between citizen and non-citizen is false. Discrimination against workers from third world countries adds yet a larger barrier to geographic borders, which already are closed enough. Our promise of international solidarity to all workers means that we cannot be apart. (López and Bonmatí 1997)

The belief that immigrants are part of the international class struggle makes restrictive immigration policies unacceptable to many labor union leaders and forms the philosophical foundation for their preferences for moderately open immigration policies.

But when immigrant workers threaten the wages and working conditions of native workers, exclusively ideological arguments in favor of moderately open immigration policies produce two dilemmas for unions. The first dilemma is whether to protect the interests of all workers or give primacy to those of union members. The second is whether to protect immigrants already present or future immigrants.

The best illustration of these dilemmas is the variance in the CGT's immigration preferences from the mid-1940s to the mid-1980s. After World War II, France experienced an economic boom and a demographic crisis. Shortages in domestic labor meant that foreign labor was needed to sustain high growth rates. The CGT had to choose between advocating its ideological position of working-class internationalism, or taking the more narrow position of protecting French workers.

Early in its history, the CGT developed an antagonistic relationship with the state by espousing revolutionary Marxist ideology, syndicalism, and the General Strike. CGT leadership saw immigration as a consequence of the capitalist regime's need to ensure a plentiful supply of cheap and docile workers. Although the CGT initially supported immigration, it did so under the condition of absolute equality for foreign and native workers that was guaranteed in the 1945 *ordonnance*. By 1947, however, the organization had changed its position, and opposed all immigration in an effort to protect its native constituency. This anti-immigration attitude persisted through the 1950s and the early 1960s.

However, by the late 1960s, the CGT began to gradually transform its immigration preferences as it recognized the inevitability of immigration flows under the economic and demographic circumstances existing in France. No longer rejecting immigration, the organization instead demanded that the state better organize foreign labor recruitment, which by the late 1960s was largely controlled by employers who recruited immigrants illegally. In 1969, the CGT held a national conference to plan how to defend and organize immigrant workers. The program that emerged from the conference called for all foreign labor recruitment to be carried out by the National Immigration Office (ONI) with trade union participation, and for more legal guarantees ensuring equal rights for immigrant and native workers.

In 1971, the CGT and CFDT issued a joint statement that makes clear their internationalist stance. "We believe that immigrant workers are an integral part of the working-class and are not competitive with French workers. We intend to locate our actions with and for immigrant workers within the general framework of the struggle for all workers" (Freeman 1978, 33).

The CGT's more favorable attitude toward immigration in the early 1970s led it to oppose the 1972 Marcellin-Fontenet administrative orders, which called for more restrictive policies toward illegal immigrants and linked recruitment more closely to labor needs. The CGT argued that these policies would place immigrants in a vulnerable and unequal position relative to native workers.

But just two years later, in another major change of position, the CGT supported the 1974 suspension of employment-based immigration. CGT leadership felt that the economic crisis would be short-lived and that the suspension was necessary to help resolve it. Although the CGT feared that the suspension might alienate foreign workers, it wanted a policy that would reestablish state control over immigration policy. According to Gérard Chemouil, the organization's representative for immigration, it took ten years for the CGT to realize that the economic crisis of the early 1970s was not short-term, and that supporting the halt on immigration contradicted its own ideology and efforts to help immigrant workers in France (author interview, September 18, 1997).

Although the CGT has a strong working-class ideology, its changing preferences signal the failure of exclusively ideological arguments to explain why unions defend open immigration policies. If ideology alone determined preferences, then we would not expect such frequent shifts in position from a union with such a strong internationalist, working-class history. Nor would we expect a union founded on the principles of anticommunism, Catholicism, and the rejection of class conflict, such as the Confederazione Italiana Sindicati Lavoratori (CISL), to be a leading immigrant organization in Italy. Consistently, the CISL has supported moderately open immigration policies, including a regular legalization process for illegal immigrants and more expansive quotas. CISL leadership bases its support for such policies on the belief that immigration to Italy is a new and irreversible phenomenon. Consequently, the leadership believes that Italians and immigrants should have equal social, economic, and political rights and equal access to membership in the CISL.

In fact, according to Gérard Chemouil, an exclusively ideological position is not central to CGT's immigration policy preferences.

> It is false to separate the ideological goals of the union from the practi-
> cal ones . . . . an exclusively ideological position hurts unions because it
> marginalizes their ability to influence government policies and ostra-
> cizes workers that do not agree with the union ideology. (author inter-
> view, September 18, 1997)

Victor Gomez, a lawyer with the Comisiones Obreras (CCOO),
agrees that the ideological explanation is not as relevant today as it was
in the past. To better understand labor leaders' stance on immigration,
it is necessary to address how globalization has hindered states' capacity to control immigration effectively, changed the dynamics of labor
union organization and membership, and stimulated the growth of the
underground economy.

Doubting the State's Capacity to Control Immigration

> Neither the state nor the European Union can stop the flow of immi-
> grants to France. In fact, national borders are becoming increasingly
> meaningless in the EU. (Author interview, François Srocynski, Repre-
> sentative for Immigration, CFDT, Paris, September 17, 1997)

> Italian immigration law is one of the most restrictive in Europe on con-
> trolling flows. It is almost impossible to enter Italy legally, but the ap-
> plication of the law is very poor. (Author interview, Angelo Masetti,
> National Representative for Migration, UIL, Rome, December 3, 1997)

The efficient functioning of the market requires free international exchange of goods, money, and people, which often challenges a state's
capacity to control national economic policy, labor markets, and borders. On the other hand, states often interfere with the market to promote the national interest through trade, investment, and immigration
policies. During much of the nineteenth century the market functioned
with little state interference. For example, passports and work permits
often were not required for migration within Europe. However, protec-

tionism, war, and depression prevailed in the first half of the twentieth century, effectively closing international markets.

Compared to the free market that preceded World War I, today's global marketplace is more inclusive and moving at a quicker technological pace. More developed and developing states participate in it. Globalization is driven by rapid changes in technology, such as cheap and efficient communication networks that allow firms to locate different parts of their production process in different countries. More accessible communication technology also reduces the need for personal contact between producers and consumers, facilitating trade in services. Finally, gross international financial flows are much greater than in the nineteenth century.

The global market for labor is relatively underdeveloped, however, compared to the global markets for goods, services, and money. In developing countries the encroaching global market has helped stimulate migration, but states still largely influence migration patterns through rules governing entry and exit. Unlike free trade, which is built on firm international institutional foundations, for migration no comprehensive international regime exists. Until the recent decision by the member states of the European Union to coordinate immigration policy, states found it more effective to unilaterally impose immigration policies than to coordinate on an international level.[1]

Nonetheless, many government officials in receiving states are concerned about an "immigration control crisis," and have less confidence in their ability to effectively regulate immigration flows and the employment of illegal workers than they did fifteen years ago. Cornelius, Martin, and Hollifield (1994) articulate the conflict between states and the market concerning migration as a "gap" between policies to control immigration and immigration outcomes. This gap between policies and outcomes is a result of pressures emanating from outside the state, such as the expansion of transnational migration networks aided by advances in communication and

---

[1] Under the Amsterdam Treaty (1997) competency for immigration policy within the EU will gradually be transferred from intergovernmental institutions to Community institutions.

transportation technology. When states restrict labor migration, these networks help sustain flows through family reunification and illegal immigration. A second exogenous factor is increasing economic openness among developing countries, which in the short run accentuates social and economic imbalances and encourages emigration.

Labor leaders are cognizant of the difficulties states have in controlling immigration. Given the inevitability of immigration, labor leaders believe that they are taking a rational position in favor of moderately open immigration policies, because they are convinced that restrictive policies only serve to increase the precariousness of immigrant workers, which hurts both immigrant and native workers. On the other hand, labor leaders believe that such moderate policies as legalization of illegal immigrants, permanent residency, and family reunification increase the stability of immigrant workers.

> UGT does not want totally open immigration policy but realizes that immigration will continue regardless of government efforts to control it. Therefore, UGT favors policies that encourage legal immigration such as family reunification, regularization, free movement of legal immigrants within the EU and permanent residency. (Author interview, Ana Maria Corral Juan, Representative for Immigration, UGT, Madrid, October 10, 1997)

> CCOO takes a rational position that immigration will continue despite European or Spanish efforts to stop it. CCOO defends the rights of immigrant workers in Spain and promotes family reunification, regularization and permanent residency. (Author interview, Victor Gomez, immigration lawyer, CCOO, Madrid, October 29, 1997)

In addition to international constraints, domestic factors limit a state's ability control its borders and further shape labor leaders' preferences. For example, Italy's former policy of not detaining illegal immigrants, combined with corruption in the underground economy, made controlling illegal immigration impossible. According to one Italian labor leader, employer sanctions are not enforced because the government benefits from profits made in the underground economy and, in the south, threats made by employers often discourage labor inspectors from interfering in illegal enterprises (author interview, Angelo Masetti, National Representative for Migration, UIL, Rome, December

3, 1997). Hence, Italian labor leaders favor policies that promote legal immigration while meeting employers' demand for immigrant workers, such as employment-based quotas and legalization. In one southern Spanish province, a subsidy paid to Spanish agricultural workers three months out of the year, combined with undesirable working conditions under plastic sheeting, discourages Spaniards from working during the summer months. As a result of acute summer labor shortages, many employers recruit illegal immigrants from North Africa. Because these agricultural enterprises are family-owned and highly decentralized, local labor inspectors rarely enforce employer sanctions. Therefore, a poorly designed social welfare benefit together with decentralized businesses makes controlling illegal immigration in this province difficult. As a result, provincial labor leaders have lobbied the local government to secure increases from the central government for the provincial immigration quota.

These examples illustrate labor leaders' lack of confidence in the efficacy of restrictive policies given global and domestic constraints on the state's ability to control immigration. However, this was not always the case. As we saw, up to the mid-1980s French labor leaders were much more confident in the state's ability to control immigration. They frequently petitioned the ONI to better control immigration flows, and state-directed immigration worked reasonably well until the early 1960s, when employers began increasingly to recruit immigrant labor independently of the state, legalizing immigrant workers after they arrived in France. By the late 1960s legalization rates had reached 80 percent, indicating that the ONI had lost control over regulating flows. Nonetheless, in 1969 the CGT once again called on the ONI to take immigration out of employers' control. Again in 1974, many labor leaders supported the government suspension of labor immigration, certain that stopping immigration would improve the unemployment situation. However, by the early 1980s thousands of illegal immigrants were employed in the underground economy, and French labor leaders were much less confident about the state's ability to control immigration.

In promoting more moderate immigration policies, labor leaders run the risk of ostracizing those workers who feel threatened by immigrants. Consequently, labor leaders in France, Italy, and Spain are trying to educate workers about the costs of highly restrictive immigration policies, which marginalize immigrant workers and undercut the wages and protections of all workers. By supporting policies that advance legal immigration, labor unions stand to gain organizationally through greater access to government funds for immigrants and to the immigration policy-making process. Also, immigrants are a potential new source of membership for unions. Finally, by supporting policies that improve immigrant stability, such as the legalization of illegal immigrants, labor unions bring part of the underground economy to the surface.

Union Organization: Immigrants as a New Source of Strength

Globalization can be expected to have a deleterious effect on labor union membership rates for several reasons. Increased openness to international competition may reduce the ability of unions to deliver higher wages to their members. With fewer benefits to union membership, workers will be less likely to join. Global economic competition may induce employers to seek a union-free environment to reduce costs and increase flexibility (Lange and Scruggs 1998, 5). And growing economic insecurity may discourage workers from joining unions and paying the cost of union membership. If globalization does hurt unions, then we should see declining union membership rates in countries open to trade and capital flows. However, the empirical evidence that globalization directly affects union density has been inconclusive. Recent studies show that domestic institutions intervene between global economic forces and union density rates, so that density rates across countries are in fact diverging. In countries that had low union density rates at the start of the 1970s, membership rates have continued to decline, while unions in high density countries have become stronger.

France and Spain qualify as low union density countries. France, with a membership rate of 21.5 percent in 1970, ranked last among industrialized countries; in 1989, it was still last and the rate had fallen to 10.2 percent. Spain also experienced a rapid decline in union membership in the 1980s. Immediately after the Spanish transition to democracy in 1976, unions were legalized and unionization rates soared to almost 45 percent of the workforce. Thereafter, however, rates fell sharply, to 20 percent in 1982, and today are around 10 percent. Italy, on the other hand, experienced a slight increase in union density rates between 1970 and 1989. In 1970, Italy was ranked eleventh among industrialized countries with an unionization rate of 33.4 percent. In 1989, it had risen to ninth, with 33.5 percent of the workforce unionized (Lange and Scruggs 1998, 8).

Despite the ambiguity of the academic literature, most French, Italian, and Spanish labor union leaders feel threatened by the effects of increasing global economic competition. Most unions are searching for new forms of organization and reaching out to new kinds of workers. Immigrants, women, young people, pensioners, and the unemployed are all sources of relatively untapped membership for unions. As a result, Spanish, Italian, and French unions have developed institutions and programs that incorporate immigrants' interests into the union and address specific problems faced by immigrants.

Yet despite these institutions and programs, the Spanish and French unions have found it difficult to attract immigrant members. One often cited reason for low affiliation rates among immigrants is their precarious, short-term status and their shifting between legal and underground employment. Also, like native workers, legally employed immigrants enjoy many of the benefits of union membership without having to join because, by law, collective bargaining agreements cover all workers regardless of union membership. Finally, the Spanish unions provide free legal and professional services to immigrants regardless of their affiliation with a union. The proportion of the immigrant workforce affiliated with French and Spanish unions is even lower than among native workers. Nevertheless, by organizing around the issue of immigration, the French and Spanish unions have gained access to the policy-making process and to government funding for immigrant programs.

In Italy, where overall unionization rates are close to 40 percent, immigrant affiliation rates are also high.[2] Approximately 105,000 immi-

---

[2] Overall unionization rates include pensioners, who make up 54.5 percent of CGIL membership, 47.4 percent of CISL membership, and 23.2 percent of UIL membership (Bedani 1995, 329).

grants are affiliated with the CISL, 72,000 with the CGIL and 20,000 with the UIL. The unique Italian model of parallel immigrant union organization and securing leadership positions for immigrants has afforded labor leaders a powerful voice for affecting immigration policies.

The French, Italian, and Spanish unions have organized around the issue of immigration in three ways. The first model of immigrant organization I call the assimilationist, French model. The second is the social service, Spanish model. And, the third is the parallel union, Italian model. The only exception to these distinctions by country is the Italian CGIL, which has adopted a mix of the Spanish and French models.

The French Model: Assimilating Immigrants into the Union

The French model of union organization has been shaped by the French traditions of equality and assimilation. Also, the French model has been influenced by the highly developed institutional framework of government agencies dedicated to immigration and a plethora of nongovernmental associations that provide social and legal services to immigrants. This extensive network allows labor unions to focus on labor market issues of concern to immigrants. Consequently, the French model for immigrant organization is unitary and focused on workplace issues.

On the one hand, by addressing immigrant workers' interests as part of a larger class struggle, French unions helped the first wave of immigrants integrate into French society and gain workplace rights. On the other hand, the assimilationist model has distanced the unions from problems faced by illegal immigrant workers and second-generation immigrants, who are on the margins of the workforce. According to Claude Valentine Marie, Head of Research for the French Mission to Fight against Clandestine Work, French unions have been unable to change their way of thinking about workers in the new global economy and about how to incorporate these workers into the union.

After experimenting with language groupings for immigrant workers at the local level, the CGT rejected the concept of separate organizations for immigrants. Wary that addressing the concerns of immigrants through separate union structures would divide workers, the French unions have tried to deal with the immigrants' interests within the larger framework of workers' interests. For example, in the early 1980s the trade unions tried to incorporate the religious demands of Muslim workers, such as prayer rooms and reduced working hours during Ramadan, into a defense of workers' freedom of thought. According to Catherine Withol de Wenden (1988), the unions incorporated religion into general union concerns through a "catch-all" strategy conducted in the name of respect for cultural identities and dignity.

In her study of the disputes in the French car industry between 1981 and 1983 at Renault's Billancourt plant, Withol de Wenden delineated three strategies by which the unions incorporated the demands of Muslim workers. The first position, adopted by the CFDT, was to separate religious demands from work-related demands. The CFDT's policy was to integrate immigrant workers by playing down Islam but at the same time respecting the religious autonomy of workers. The second position, adopted by the CGT, was to reluctantly defend the demands of Muslim workers for prayer time when it became an issue of health and safety. The third position, also adopted by the CGT, was to mobilize workers in the name of religious demands fearing that if it did not, it would lose control over the situation. None of these strategies attempted to isolate or separate Muslim workers. Instead, they sought to incorporate and integrate Muslim workers into the union.

Today the CGT, CFDT, and FO are pursuing campaigns to fight racism in the workplace. In much the same way as they did in the 1980s, the unions are addressing the issue of racism as a scourge that undermines the workers' common struggle. Many labor leaders believe that racism, transformed into policies that discriminate against immigrants, can undermine the common goals of all workers. For example:

> The right-wing National Front party does not want immigrants to receive social security benefits. Because the social security system is in deficit, the National Front believes it should be reserved for French workers. However, if one group of workers is excluded, the ability of all workers to receive benefits will be undermined. (Author interview, Gérard Chemouil, Representative for Immigration, CGT, Paris, September 18, 1997).

The CFDT is fighting racism in the workplace through a strategy that seeks to gain the support of all members through a gradual, educational approach to studying and teaching militants and workers about the problems of racism. The CFDT's three-part strategy to integrate immigrants is to make it easier for immigrants to obtain jobs, housing, and citizenship (CFDT 1997). The FO, the union with the smallest immigrant membership, has also joined in the fight against racism on a much smaller scale than the other two. An FO study of workplace racism in Paris and Yvelines revealed that it is a problem; but, most union militants feel that they lack the time to deal with complex problems of racism. Subsequently, the FO initiated a training program for local activists in Paris and Yvelines.

How has the French model affected labor leaders' preferences? First, the French unions have taken a back seat in policy discussions that concern controlling the entry of immigrants. Most labor leaders believe these pure immigration issues are outside the scope of the unions and, within the unions, support for immigration is weak and divided. Nevertheless, many labor leaders support family reunification, permanent residency, and legalization. Second, labor leaders have focused on issues of racism and discrimination, which encompass immigrant as well as native workers. By adopting this approach, the French unions are trying to nurture a more global perspective toward immigration among the rank and file.

The Spanish Model: Unions as Social Service Providers for Immigrants

The Spanish model of union organization around immigration has been shaped by Spain's history of emigration and by the lack of associationalism in Spanish society. Between 1940 and the late 1960s, millions of Spaniards emigrated to northern Europe and Latin America. Today, approximately 3 million Spaniards are still abroad. The Spanish labor unions, especially the CCOO, have supported Spanish workers abroad and their repatriation to Spain. For example, in its first Congress in 1977, the CCOO created a Secretariat for Emigration, which was transformed into the Secretariat for Emigration and Immigration in 1987.

In the mid-1980s, when immigrants first started to arrive in Spain in significant numbers, there was a dearth of support services for them.

Labor unions were one of the few nongovernmental organizations with migration experience, and the CCOO quickly moved to fill the void. In 1986, it opened its first Centro de Información para Trabajadores Extranjeros (Information Center for Foreign Workers or CITE) to provide legal, social, and educational services to immigrants. Today both the CCOO and the UGT have national networks of offices that deal specifically with the legal and professional needs of immigrant workers.

Also influencing the way the unions have organized themselves around the issue of immigration is the neocorporatist system of negotiated pacts among the state, labor unions, and employers that helped transform Spain into a democracy in late 1970s and early 1980s. In this system the state became the most powerful actor and the primary decision-maker, but consultations with labor and business also were ingrained into all aspects of labor relations, including immigration. For instance, the Ministry of the Interior and Ministry of Labor meet regularly with labor and business leaders to consult on annual quotas. The government has also relied on labor unions to provide many social services to immigrants because it was unprepared and poorly organized to meet their needs. It was not until the mid-1990s that the Ministries of Labor and Interior developed agencies that provide services to immigrants. Therefore, labor unions became one of the main providers of social, legal, and educational services for immigrants and have been one of the main beneficiaries of state funding for immigrant programs.

Consequently, the Spanish labor unions have organized themselves around the issue of immigration as social service agencies. In 1997, the CCOO had over a hundred CITE offices throughout Spain, and the UGT had established eleven Centros Guias para Inmigrantes y Refugiados (Advisory Centers for Immigrants and Refugees) in regions most heavily populated with immigrants. The CITE and Centro Guia offices provide immigrants with free legal services concerning regularization procedures, family reunification, and how to obtain work permits, residency permits, and visas. They have initiated campaigns on the local level to promote immigrants' rights. For example, CITE and Centro Guia representatives were active in the campaigns to regularize immigrants in 1991 and 1996. Finally, these local offices provide language and professional training to immigrants. CITE and Centro Guia are not membership organizations, and to use their services an immigrant does not have to be a member of the union or even a legal immigrant.

Immigrants who wish to join the CCOO and UGT must affiliate directly with the unions. Data gathered by CITE offices reveals that there is a demand for the services of the CITE but not necessarily a strong interest in joining the CCOO. In 1994, there were some 101,977 legally employed immigrant workers in Spain. In that same year, 25,856 immigrants used the services of CITE offices some 60,734 times. In 1995, there were 68,744 total consultations in CITE offices. However, in 1994 only 8,856 immigrants were members of the CCOO. In 1995, the CCOO estimated close to 11,000 immigrant members. Immigrant unionization rates are even lower in the UGT. Union leadership attributes low membership rates to the precarious, often illegal, short-term work done by most immigrant workers, and the institutionalized irregularity built into the system of short-term work and residency permits. However, affiliating immigrant workers is not the main goal of union leadership. Instead, they want to increase the security and stability of immigrant workers in Spain in the belief that the exploitation of immigrant workers places native workers in a worse situation for maintaining and improving social achievements. With this in mind, both unions have conducted several information campaigns to pressure the government to reform the systems for legalization, permit renewals, and family reunification.

Contributing to this social service model of union organization is government funding for immigrant programs that began in 1986. Total funding for immigrant programs grew substantially, from 36,098,163 pesetas in 1986 to a high of 378,987,057 pesetas in 1995. A wide range of programs have been funded including employment training, language training, housing, promoting multiculturalism and preventing racism, and academic research on immigration. As Table 1 shows, labor unions have been an important beneficiary of government funding for labor-related programs. Other recipients of government funding include Caritas, immigrant associations, the Red Cross, universities, and local governments.

In the early 1990s, the increase in funding for immigrant programs and the opening of institutional access through bodies such as the Forum for the Integration of Immigrants encouraged unions to become

Table 1. Spanish government funding for immigrant programs

Year	Total funding (pesetas)	Percent of funds for labor programs	Percent of labor funds to unions
1990	103,204,000	31	11
1991	218,618,462	46	49
1992	347,970,266	86	30
1993	367,971,000	n/a	n/a
1994	367,787,057	48	53
1995	378,987,057	23	16
1996	346,463,000	21	40

Source: Ministry of Labor and Social Affairs (1996)

more involved on questions of immigration. According to Francisco Soriano, the former Director of Migration for the CCOO, the unions have used the major part of their government funding to provide legal services to immigrants, to offer professional training programs, and to conduct information campaigns on immigrants' rights. Without government funding, many of the services provided by the unions would not exist.

By filling an institutional gap and providing legal, professional, and educational services to immigrants the CCOO and UGT have become experts on immigration. For example, at an October 1997 meeting of the Forum for the Integration of Immigrants, attended by nongovernmental organization, immigrant associations, employers, and government officials, the unions dominated discussions concerning the quota for 1997 and reforming the quota policy. At the meeting, the UGT representative presented a proposal, written by the unions and supported by the nongovernmental associations, to reform the quota policy, making it easier for immigrants to come to Spain and providing a means for undocumented immigrants already in Spain to legalize their situation.

The grassroots, social service approach of the Spanish labor unions has helped shape their preferences for moderately open immigration policies and made the unions a leading advocate for immigrants. Hence, the labor unions want a faster, simpler process for obtaining work and residency permits and access to long-term work and residency permits, including permanent residency status. Also, the unions have demanded eased restrictions on family reunification and a regular legalization procedure for undocumented immigrants who have jobs in

Spain. Finally, Spain's experience with emigration has endowed the unions with a global perspective toward migration as well as internal organizations oriented to the needs of emigrants and immigrants.

The Italian Model: Parallel Union Organization for Immigrants

How Italian unions have organized around the issue of immigration has been shaped by forces similar to those in Spain: the national experience with emigration, weak associationalism in society, and a lack of government capacity to address the needs of immigrants. Italy's largest union, the CGIL, has developed a network of local offices that provide legal and social services to immigrants. The CGIL's first Ufficio Straneri (Foreigners Office) was created in 1982 to provide assistance to seasonal workers from Eastern Europe. Italy's other two unions, the CISL and UIL, also have local offices dedicated to helping immigrants.

Unique to the Italian model is the parallel immigrant membership organizations established by the UIL and CISL. Illegal and unemployed immigrants may become members of these parallel organizations because they are officially independent of the unions. But, at the same time, these parallel organizations receive funding from the UIL and CISL, and are seen as a stepping stone for immigrant membership in the unions. CISL and UIL leaders believe the parallel union structure better promotes organization and solidarity among immigrant workers, who have little experience with union democracy.

In 1988, the UIL formed its union for immigrant workers called the Unione Italiana Immigrati (UNITI). UNITI's mandate is to organize immigrant workers, train immigrants in union democracy, and provide legal and professional services. UNITI represents all immigrants, including those who are illegal, unemployed, or working without a contract. When an immigrant obtains a formal contract he or she can become a member of the UIL. In 1997, UNITI had approximately 15,000 members, concentrated in Sicily, Latium, Calabria, Veneto, and Lombardy. In 1998, the UIL's National Department for Migration Policies began to work with UNITI to grant greater autonomy to the latter's field offices. This decentralization of authority was meant to free up energies and capacities at the grassroots level. The strategy has been well received by immigrant workers, as is reflected in an increase in UNITI's membership to 50,000 in 2000 (author interview, Angelo Masetti, National Representative for Migration, UIL, November 28, 2000).

In 1989, the CISL adopted the parallel union model with the creation of the Associazione Nazionale oltre le Frontiere (ANOLF). ANOLF's three main functions are: to provide legal, professional, and educational services to immigrant workers; to promote activities in the immigrants' countries of origin; and to promote solidarity between immigrants and Italian workers through cultural and social activities. Membership in ANOLF is also open to all immigrants. ANOLF has approximately 46,000 members, and total immigrant membership in the CISL is 105,000.

The CGIL rejected the concept of a parallel union organization for immigrants. However, in 1990, it established a representative body for immigrants at the confederal level called the Coordinamento Immigrati. Initially, only immigrants were represented on the Coordinamento Immigrati, which dealt with the specific concerns and problems of immigrant workers, who could make proposals directly to the CGIL's Executive Council. However, often these proposals were not taken seriously by the Executive Council because they did not represent the union as a whole. In addition, many of the proposals dealt with social issues such as housing and health care rather than employment-related issues (author interview, Adriana Buffardi, President, IRES-CGIL, Rome, December 16, 1997). In early 1997, the Coordinamento Immigrati was reorganized and made into a more representative body with both Italians and immigrants on its board. Under the new structure, the Coordinamento Immigrati can no longer present proposals directly to the Executive Council, and it is more focused on work-related issues such as training, professional mobility, and recognition of diplomas from other countries. Hence, the CGIL is moving closer to the French model, with the belief that it is detrimental to separate the interests of immigrants from other workers. At the same time, it has also retained the social service aspects of the Spanish model through its network of local service offices for immigrants. The CGIL has approximately 72,000 immigrant members (Faye 2000).

The CGIL also stresses the participation of immigrants in leadership positions. For example, it requires that a percentage of shop stewards be immigrants. Shop stewards participate at the regional level of the

CGIL, serving as a conduit between national-level decision-making and local collective bargaining.

Clearly, the Italian experience with emigration and the void in social services for immigrants have been important factors in how the CGIL, CISL, and UIL have organized around the issue of immigration as social service providers. In fact, a representative from the Ministry of Social Solidarity confirmed that the government has relied extensively on the unions to provide many social and legal services to immigrants (author interview, Vaifra Palanca, Assistant to Minister Livia Turco, Ministry of Social Solidarity, Rome, December 5, 1997). However, what factors explain the unique parallel union organization of the CISL and UIL?

One factor is the founding principle of anticommunism shared by the two unions. Another factor is the high percentage of immigrants originating from communist and former communist countries such as Albania, which provides the second largest group of immigrants in Italy (6.1 percent); the former Yugoslavia accounts for 4 percent, Romania for 2.9, and China and Poland each for 2.5 (Caritas di Roma 1997, 54). A third factor is the overwhelming number of illegal immigrants working in the underground economy, who are not eligible to join the main union organizations because they do not have formal work contracts.

In 1950, internal divisions within the communist-based CGIL led to the creation of two new unions, the exclusively Catholic CISL and the non-secular, anticommunist UIL. American labor leaders influenced the founding of the CISL and UIL as part of America's Cold War initiative. The CISL adopted a mix of American labor and Catholic ideas, which included a focus on plant-level negotiations and working with management to industrialize and modernize the Italian economy. The Catholic influence led to the rejection of the notion of class conflict and acceptance of the idea of guided capitalism. The UIL, the weakest of the three unions, attracted republicans and socialists who refused to join a union dominated by Catholics. The UIL has followed a similar strategy of anticommunism and decentralized bargaining.

One of the main goals of ANOLF and UNITI is to educate new immigrants about union democracy. Therefore, the strong tradition of anticommunism combined with the influx of immigrants from former communist countries helps explain the parallel union structure of CISL and UIL. These parallel unions can focus on the specific needs of immigrant workers and on the appropriate orientation to union democracy to prepare them for membership in the CISL and UIL. Also contributing to the development of parallel unions are the large numbers of illegal immigrant workers who could not otherwise join a union. Illegal immigrants can join ANOLF and UNITI because they are constituted as immigrant organizations, instead of labor unions, which are open only to legal workers.

Because of this unique parallel organization structure and the social services they provide to immigrants, the CGIL, CISL, and UIL all favor moderately open immigration policies that make it easier for immigrants to obtain work and residency permits, regularize their status, and bring their families to Italy. For example, the Italian unions lobbied for the inclusion of a special quota in the 1998 immigration law that would allow the unions to sponsor immigrants. Under the sponsor quota, labor unions can bring immigrants to Italy if they guarantee employment and housing.

Attempts to Bring the Underground Economy to the Surface

The growth of the underground economy and its connection to illegal immigration trouble labor union leaders. Employment opportunities in the underground economy attract illegal immigrants despite the risks of expulsion because the immigrants face fewer opportunities and worse living standards in their country of origin. In a March 1998 survey published in the Moroccan weekly *Le Journal*, nearly 90 percent of Moroccans in their twenties said they wanted to leave. Reasons given for emigration included "high unemployment rates, flagrant social marginalization and inequalities, which grow unceasingly."

In Spain and Italy, underground economic activity makes up 25 percent of GDP. In France, the figure is closer to 15 percent (*Economist* 1997, 63). The presence of inexpensive illegal immigrant labor encourages some employers to sink capital into the underground economy, where they can avoid the labor regulations, taxes, and high wages of the formal economy. Consequently, when employers transfer resources to the underground economy it hurts the wages and working conditions of all workers (see Dell'Aringa and Neri 1987; Djajic 1997).

Many labor leaders believe that illegal immigration and the growth of the underground economy are positively correlated. At the same time, they realize that illegal immigration is not the cause of the underground economy. For example, the proportion of illegal immigrants employed underground in France is only 2.5 percent of the total underground workforce. Rather than sacrificing the high wages and protections that have made primary labor markets inflexible, labor leaders want to regulate the underground economy and bring its workers and employers to the surface.

One way to accomplish these goals is to increase the costs and risks of employing illegal immigrants through employer sanctions. As the costs of employing illegal immigrants increases, some employers will replace these workers with native and legal immigrant workers. Indeed, labor leaders advocate stiffer employer sanctions, under the condition that illegal immigrants are not deported.

Another way is to legalize illegal immigrant workers with the requirement that they find legal employment. Once in the legal labor market, immigrant workers who entered illegally will not be preferred over native workers because of their cost effectiveness. Many labor leaders support amnesties on the economic grounds that they help both native and immigrants workers by regulating the underground economy.

However, by trying to regulate the underground economy through legalization, labor unions create the same inflexible labor market conditions that forced employers to go underground in the first place. Hence, the unions are caught in a vicious circle, in which legalization is only a temporary solution to deeply embedded structural problems of labor market segmentation. The foundations for labor market segmentation were laid in the postwar period when powerful labor unions negotiated high wages and generous benefits for workers in exchange for control over production decisions. In the late 1970s and 1980s, labor market segmentation came to fruition as a result of increasing global competition and the drive for European employers to compete with Asian and American markets.

In the late 1960s, the "hot autumns" of labor unrest in France and Italy resulted in grand bargains among the state, employers, and unions. Taking a conciliatory position, the state and employers accepted wage increases and job protection to avoid the costs of further worker unrest. In France sweeping labor legislation called the Grenelle Accords was passed in 1969. In Italy, the 1970 Statuto dei Lavoratori guaranteed workers higher wages, more benefits, and greater job security. In Spain, the legacy of Franco's rigid corporatist and protectionist policies compounded by slow economic growth between 1975 and 1981 contributed to the expansion of the underground economy. Spain's official economy was unable to create enough jobs for the large numbers of women and young people who entered the workforce and were no longer willing to emigrate. Adding to Spain's labor market inflexibility were labor regulations, introduced in the 1970s, called the Ordenanza Laborales, that made it difficult for employers to fire workers.

Into the mid-1970s, the states tried to guarantee full employment and union influence over unemployment insurance, pensions, health insurance, and training programs in return for labor quiescence and moderate wage demands. But the crisis of the welfare state and the growing interdependence of national economies constrained fiscal policy and limited the governments' ability to deliver on their end of the bargain. At the same time, employers were searching for new ways to organize production to compete with low-wage, less-regulated Asian and Latin American markets.

In the short run, the labor unions gained broad protections and high wages for many workers. However, in this trade-off, employers retained control over production decisions. As the period of economic growth and full employment of the 1960s gave way to economic recession and unemployment in the 1970s and 1980s, labor unions faced the negative effects of their trade-off with employers and the state. First, employers gained access to more flexible labor resources through reforms in the labor law. For example, in 1984, Spanish employers were given the right to hire workers on fixed-term contracts. By 1997, nearly a third of Spanish workers were on temporary contracts. Second, employers have found ways to circumvent labor laws and unions by creating microenterprises that are extremely difficult for unions to organize. For example, the Statuto dei Lavoratori increased job security for workers in firms with more than fourteen employees. Today, microenterprises make up 51 percent of firms in Italy (OECD 1997c, 19). Finally, some employers have turned to the underground economy.

The underground economy (also called black, clandestine, hidden, informal, irregular, shadow, and subterranean) is pervasive and growing throughout Western Europe as increasing global competition has forced employers to seek alternatives to highly regulated, inflexible labor markets.

The underground economy is part of a growing secondary economy, which includes agriculture, construction, restaurant and hotel services, domestic service, and some labor-intensive manufacturing such as clothing. Production is uncertain in the secondary sector because of economic fluctuations and changes in weather and tastes. Production also tends to be labor-intensive, seasonal, and lacking in economies of scale.

As several immigration scholars have noted, among them Portes (1983), Piore (1979), and Cheng and Bonacich (1984), the precarious status of many immigrants makes them well suited for secondary sector jobs. Spanish immigration quotas indeed channel immigrants into specific sectors, regions, and firms that face labor shortages, most importantly agriculture and domestic service.

The secondary economy is less regulated than the primary or formal economy because firms are smaller and more decentralized, making their activities more difficult to monitor. Much of the activity in the secondary economy is legal and technically covered by collective bargaining agreements, which by law include nonunionized workers and firms. However, many employers avoid regulations by taking advantage of loopholes in labor legislation and not adhering to collective bargaining agreements. As a result, workers in the secondary economy are typically not really protected by labor laws or collective bargaining agreements, nor are they unionized. Thus, these workers are considered "outsiders" compared to the "insiders" in the primary economy, who represent labor unions' core constituency.

The primary economy is shrinking as the search for labor-saving technologies replaces workers with capital, and as workers on permanent contracts are replaced with workers on temporary and part-time contracts. Also, large firms increasingly subcontract work to small firms that operate outside labor laws, collective bargaining agreements, and union organization.

Studies on how immigration is connected to the growth of the secondary economy and overall welfare have yielded varying results. For example, low-wage immigrant workers help increase profits in labor-intensive industries by lowering labor costs. But in the long run, productivity suffers as employers become reliant on immigrant labor and fail to mechanize production. More important from the perspective of unions is how an influx of unskilled immigrants affects the welfare of skilled and unskilled workers. When insulated by segmented labor markets, skilled workers benefit from immigrant labor that produces intermediate goods at a lower cost for the primary economy (see Piore 1979 and Cheng and Bonacich 1984). Unskilled workers' welfare also may improve as unskilled immigrants, who tend to occupy the lowest rung of the employment ladder, allow unskilled native workers to advance.

However, because production costs can be reduced by employing low-wage immigrant labor, an increase in the number of precarious immigrants may encourage firms to move some resources to the underground economy, given capital mobility across sectors. Dell'Aringa and Neri (1987) estimate that illegal immigrants receive a net wage 20–30 percent lower than the legal wage for the same job. On top of the lower wage, employers can evade tax and social security payments, which in Italy amount to 50 to 60 percent of basic pay (Dell' Aringa and Neri 1987, 98). Therefore, precarious immigrant workers may directly lower wages and cause job losses among unskilled native workers. Or, by encouraging employers to sink resources into the underground economy, immigrants may indirectly compete with unskilled workers in the secondary economy through a kind of displacement-wage effect (see Cheng and Bonacich 1984 and Dell'Aringa and Neri 1987). As capital is transferred to the underground economy, where wages and working conditions are generally worse than in the official economy, part of the legally employed workforce moves with it. Precarious immigrant workers in the secondary economy are most threatening to women, young people, and return migrants. These groups often prefer part-time work characteristic of the secondary economy, or lack the work experience and skill level necessary for employment in the primary labor market. Illegal immigrants may directly lower wages and cause job losses among unskilled native workers by depressing the marginal production of all workers (Chiswick 1988, 106).

Michael Piore provides a useful description of the ultimate potential effect of low-paid immigrants on the primary economy. He argues that when production costs in the underground economy fall significantly below legal production costs, the underground economy will not only absorb production from the secondary economy but may expand into the primary sector (Piore 1979, 42). Under these circumstances, the job security of even the "insiders" in the primary sector may be threatened.

Labor union leaders realize that restricting immigration does not address the fundamental problem of segmented labor markets. In fact, by restricting legal immigration the state may encourage illegal immigration. On the other hand, moderate immigration policies, such as legalization and permanent residency, help to stabilize the situation of immigrants and bring them out of the underground economy.

Once legalized, an immigrant worker is required by law to leave the underground economy and obtain official employment. However, the results of European amnesties have often been a disappointment in terms of numbers legalized and the size of reduction achieved in the underground economy. The first large European amnesty was in France in 1981–1983. The CGT, CFDT, and FO supported the amnesty because they believed it would reduce the number of illegal immigrants working in the underground economy. However, according to Bruno Quemada, Representative for Immigration for the FO, the amnesty was a failure because it did not solve the problem of illegal work. Immigrants had to change jobs once they were legalized because employers no longer wanted them, and the employers simply hired new illegal immigrants or French workers off-the-books as replacements. The results of the amnesty helped to disprove the popular belief that illegal immigrants made up the majority of workers in the underground economy. Because of this, French labor leaders no longer equate illegal immigration with illegal work, though they continue to support amnesties on humanitarian grounds.

In contrast to French labor leaders, Spanish and Italian leaders believe that legalization is a legitimate means to reduce the number of illegal immigrant workers in the underground economy and to bring part of it to the surface. In Spain, illegal immigrants make up 5 percent of workers in the underground economy and approximately 75 percent of immigrants from third-world countries do not have an employment contract (Solé 1997). In Italy, 14 percent of workers in the underground economy are illegal immigrants. Spanish and Italian labor leaders have been active in lobbying for and implementing legalization programs aimed to reduce the size of the underground economy and protect immigrant and native workers. They have been able to take these steps without arousing resentment from their core constituency because labor markets are sufficiently segmented so that "insiders" do not compete with immigrants.

Conclusion

Bringing the underground economy and illegal immigrants to the surface is one of many challenges labor unions face in an increasingly competitive global economy. Labor unions are also confronting losses in membership because of rising unemployment rates, more decentralized production in small firms that are difficult to organize, and a more diverse workforce on temporary and part-time contracts. One area in which unions are trying to adapt is immigration, which many labor leaders see as an inevitable consequence of globalization.

Reservations about the state's ability to control immigration through restrictive policies, combined with concerns about the perverse effects these policies have in marginalizing immigrants, help shape labor leaders' immigration policy preferences. However, these preferences are not identical cross-nationally, nor do labor leaders from the same country, but different unions, always share the same interests. This is because domestic factors intervene to shape their preferences in distinct ways. Nevertheless, most leaders prefer policies that promote legal immigration and stabilize the situation of immigrant workers. Ultimately, if immigrants can be brought out of a situation of institutionalized precariousness through moderate immigration policies, labor leaders believe unions, immigrants, and native workers will all benefit.

4

Explaining European Employers' Vague and Contradictory Immigration Preferences

I n 1997, agricultural employers in Almería, Spain asked the government to increase the provincial immigration quota from 1,115 to 5,600. At the same time, they threatened to hire illegal immigrants if the quota was not increased. These employers argued that immigrant labor was needed to meet labor shortages created by Spaniards' unwillingness to work under the stifling plastic sheeting characteristic of farming in the area. At the national level, Spain's main employers' association, the Confederación Española de Organizaciones Empresariales (CEOE), opposed an increase in the quota, arguing that in Almería more than 5,800 Spanish workers were receiving an unemployment subsidy at that time. In November 1997, the immigration quota for Almería was increased to 2,180.

It is not uncommon for sectoral or regional employers' groups to deviate from the position of national employers' associations to which they belong, since the smaller groups represent firms that depend on immigrant workers to do arduous, low-wage jobs. While regional and sectoral employers' associations make open demands for more immigrant labor, national employers' associations in France, Italy, and Spain prefer to maintain a low profile on immigration. However, this was not always the case.

Employers' immigration preferences, like those of labor leaders, have been shaped by changes in the global economy. Starting in the late 1970s, increasing economic competition from low-wage, less-regulated Asian and Latin American markets contributed to a fundamental shift in industrial organization in Western Europe. Many employers moved away from highly centralized, mass production to more decentralized and flexible employment and production strategies, such as temporary employment and subcontracting. At the same time, employer demand for immigrant labor shifted from large manufacturing and construction firms in the formal economy to decentralized, small firms in the informal economy. This shift in demand helps explain the ambiguous and often contradictory immigration preferences of employers.

For example, from the mid-1960s to the mid-1970s, the national French employers' association, the Conseil National de Patronat Français (CNPF), advocated liberal immigration policies. Rapid economic growth, combined with domestic labor shortages, created demand for immigrant labor in large firms, such as Peugeot and Renault. As a result, immigrant employment in the French auto industry grew from 28,300 in 1967 to 125,900 in 1973 (Hollifield 1992, 151). And across the French economy, foreign labor was instrumental in guaranteeing the profitability of other strategic sectors.

However, the CNPF's advocacy of liberal immigration policies came to an abrupt end in 1974 with the oil crisis and ensuing global economic recession. Since the mid-1970s, the organization has preferred to maintain a low-profile, vague position on immigration because of high unemployment and the political volatility of the immigration debate. The CNPF maintains this position despite the fact that, philosophically, it believes employers have the right to hire anyone, from any country, who is most qualified for a job (author interview, Emmanuel Julien, Director of European and International Affairs, CNPF, Paris, September 9, 1997). But the CNPF also argues that France does not need more unskilled immigrants. In addition, many of the firms that rely on immigrant labor today, such as clothing manufacturers, are not well represented by the CNPF because they are small and highly decentralized. Similarly, the national employers' organizations in Spain and Italy often refrain from taking a public stance on immigration.

In this chapter, I explore three questions. First, why do national employers' associations take an ambiguous position on immigration policy today compared to the CNPF's pro-immigration stance of the 1950s and 1960s? Second, why would regional and sectoral employers' associations reject the immigration position of the national employers' association? Third, why do the national employers' associations tolerate regional and sectoral affiliates that lobby openly for more open immigration policies?

In response to the first two questions, several factors help explain variances in employer preferences across time and space: macroeconomic conditions, microeconomic conditions and economic restructuring, and governability within employers' associations. How changing global economic conditions interact with domestic factors, such as industrial organization and the structure of employers' associations, helps answer the third question.

How Macroeconomic Conditions Influence Employer Preferences

When the economy is growing under conditions of almost full employment, most employers support immigration as a means to fill labor market gaps. In the 1960s, almost full employment meant that inputs of immigrant labor for semi-skilled and unskilled jobs were necessary to sustain economic growth. During the Italian economic miracle of the 1980s, many northern Italian manufacturing firms suffered labor shortages. In 1986, both employers and the unions demanded that a quota be written into the new immigration law, which would guarantee a sufficient number of immigrant workers to fill these vacancies. Under these positive economic conditions, employers and policy-makers perceive immigration policy in economic terms and immigrant labor as a resource for continued growth.

On the other hand, in a recession, employers are less likely to make open demands for immigrant labor. Although some employers may face labor shortages in specific sectors, a domestic surplus of unemployed workers makes appeals for immigrant labor politically unpopular. When a cycle of growth turns toward recession, and temporary immigrants choose to settle and bring their families, the focus of immigration policy turns increasingly to social and political issues such as welfare benefits for immigrants and voting rights. Employers do not consider these issue to be "company" concerns. Therefore, as immigration policy is removed from the economic arena, national employers' associations show less interest in immigration policy.

However, the demand for immigrant labor is not altogether determined at the national level by cycles of economic growth and recession. Two additional variables help explain why employer preferences diverge: decentralization of demand for immigrant labor and the ungovernability of national employers' associations.

How Microeconomic Changes Decentralized Demand for Immigrant Labor

Under the model of mass production prevalent in France during the 1950s and 1960s, demand for immigrant labor was concentrated in large firms. As a result of state-directed economic planning focused on "national champions," national employers' associations became attuned to the needs of large firms. Given domestic labor shortages, many large French manufacturing firms required immigrant labor to achieve economies of scale and reduce labor costs. Consequently, the CNPF advocated liberal immigration policies.

In the late 1960s and early 1970s labor unrest and the oil crisis challenged the system of mass production, which proved unfit to meet rapid global economic changes in the 1970s and 1980s. Wage and benefit concessions made by employers and the state to the labor unions increased labor market inflexibility. It was no longer profitable for large French firms to hire immigrant labor because of the protections won by unions for all workers. In fact, at the start of the recession in the 1970s, immigrants were the first to be laid off by the large French auto manufacturers.

However, at the margins of the economy where unions have been unable to protect workers, the areas of microenterprises and underground work, the demand for cheap immigrant labor remains. This decentralization of demand for immigrant labor has been one manifestation of a much larger economic transformation, in which employers have tried to increase profitability by making their workforce and production methods more flexible and responsive to economic changes.

How Poor Governability Explains Employers' Contradictory Immigration Preferences

The problem of governability, of unifying interests and making members comply with organizational goals, concerns compliance between the national employers' association and its affiliates, which include sectoral associations, regional associations, and individual firms. With regard to immigration, it concerns the discrepancy between the ambiguous position of the national association and the pro-immigrant stance of some regional and sectoral associations. The problem of governability in employers' organizations starts from the premise that an individual's willingness to join an organization is distinct from a willingness to comply with organizational goals.

Compared to labor unions, employers' organizations have a higher degree of associability, the capacity to recruit members, and a lower degree of governability (Traxler 1991). For example, in France the CNPF represents 85 sectoral and 150 local employers' associations, which cover 13 million of 14 million French workers in the private sector—whereas the five French labor unions combined represent about 5 percent of the private sector workforce (author interview, Emmanuel Julien, Director of European and International Affairs, CNPF, Paris, September 9, 1997). However, unlike workers, individual firms have sufficient resources to pursue their interests over the collective interests of the organization. In addition to the question of resource control, employers' associations differ from labor unions because product market interests divide employers. Consequently, firm strategies are often oriented against other firms rather than toward workers.

This asymmetry of power between the organization and its members renders employers' organizations less governable than unions. Because of intraclass competition, individual firms readily defect from associational goals when these goals are not in the firms' best interest. A firm may choose not to comply with an associational goal and still retain membership. Because individual firms control resources, it would be costly for an employers' association to sanction or expel firms that defect from organization goals.

The problem of governability helps explain how individual firms can recruit and hire illegal immigrant labor when the position of their national employers' association is, at best, ambiguous and, at times, opposed to recruiting such labor. In the case of large firms, their interests often take precedence over associational goals because they contribute the majority of financial and human resources that sustain the association. Therefore, large firms that hire illegal immigrant labor, such as Bouyghes, a French construction company, typically are not sanctioned by the CNPF (author interview, René Moriaux, Research Director, CE-VIPOF, Paris, September 11, 1997). At the same time, national employers' associations have insufficient resources to monitor whether small, highly decentralized firms are hiring illegal immigrant workers. Finally, immigration is a low priority for national employers' associations because large firms' profitability no longer depends on immigrant labor. The economic advantages for large firms of hiring immigrant workers are slight because of domestic labor surpluses and the fact that collective bargaining agreements cover almost all workers. However, the negative publicity and political consequences if national employers' associations were to lobby for open immigration policies under conditions of recession and high unemployment could be severe.

Economic Growth and Centralized Demand for Immigrant Labor

Between 1951 and 1973, the French economy flourished, with an average annual growth rate of 4.14 and near-full employment.[1] The state took an active, interventionist role in the economy as planner, investor, and owner. In the 1950s, national economic planning focused on strengthening broad sectors of the economy deemed most crucial for economic development, such as steel, coal, transport, electricity, cement, chemicals, telecommunications, and agricultural machinery. In

---

[1] Annual growth rate of real GDP per capita in 1985 international prices (ACLP World Political/ Economic Database 1995).

the 1960s, the focus of industrial policy shifted from sectors to individual firms. The state intervened by consolidating sectors and merging small firms to create industrial giants capable of competing internationally. Each year from 1966 through 1969 saw a series a mergers with a value twice that of all mergers between 1950 and 1960 (Hall 1986, 149).

During this period of economic expansion, a synergy was created between industrial policy and immigration policy. Given chronic shortages of French labor after World War II, economic planners and firms realized that immigrant labor was necessary to achieve economies of scale and rapid economic growth. Initially, immigrants were most heavily recruited in mining and construction, which absorbed a third of all immigrants entering the labor force between 1946 and 1955. In the 1960s, immigrant labor became a crucial component of economic growth in manufacturing, construction, and services. However, by the late 1960s, immigrant employment in these sectors was already declining as a result of economic slowdown and resulting layoffs (Hollifield 1992, 144).

The essential ingredients for the model of French postwar industrial development were mass production of standardized products, income stabilization policies to assure consumer demand, and work organization built on narrowly defined jobs and hierarchically organized corporations. According to this model, capital ownership would become increasingly concentrated in large firms, and small firms would gradually wither away because of inferior organization, management, and technology.

Although small firms did not wither away, large firm success became the priority of industrial policy in postwar France. As a result, the CNPF eschewed its traditional allegiance to small firms in favor of large firms. Until the mid-1960s, the CNPF maintained an ambivalent position toward national economic planning in an effort to placate large firms, which approved of national economic plans, and maintain the support of small firms, which felt threatened by government planning and made up a majority of CNPF membership. Because of the CNPF's detached position on economic planning, the state often negotiated directly with individual firms instead.

This relationship changed in the mid-1960s when Paul Huvelin succeeded Georges Villiers as CNPF president. Villiers was the owner of a small family firm who had led the organization since 1946. Huvelin, on the other hand, was managing director of a large firm. Huvelin forced through a series of reforms that established the CNPF as the voice for French industry, bringing the organization in line with industrial policy and under the control of large enterprises (Hall 1986, 168). Hence, a strong alliance was built between national economic planners, the CNPF, and large firms, with increasing the competitiveness of French firms as their top priority. Because profitability hinged on a system of mass production that relied on a steady influx of cheap unskilled and semi-skilled labor, the CNPF favored open immigration policies and backed private recruitment by individual firms.

This postwar model of economic growth seemed invincible in the 1960s, as the average annual growth rate reached 4.76. However, in the late 1960s and early 1970s, unemployment rates began to creep up, accompanied by social and economic turmoil that challenged industrial organization based on labor-intensive work and mass production.

Social and Economic Crises: Challenges to the System of Mass-Based Production

In the late 1960s and early 1970s, labor unrest and economic crisis brought on by the oil shock dramatically altered the demand for immigrant labor in France, and shaped the future demand for it in Spain and Italy.

In France, the protests of May 1968 that began among students quickly spread to factories and resulted in massive labor strikes. The impetus for social unrest sprang from a multitude of tensions in French society in areas such as education, industry, and the role of the state in economic planning. The strikes were settled through negotiations between labor and management that resulted in legislation called the Grenelle Accords. As a result, the minimum wage increased by 33 percent, with more modest wage increases at higher levels. More important, new rights were granted to labor unions at the local and national level. For example, workers were granted the right to organize in the workplace and to work through their representatives in the firm to oversee and restrain managerial action. Also, the Grenelle Accords tightened legal restraints on employers' freedom to lay off workers for economic reasons.

The Grenelle Accords set off a brief period of rapid economic expansion fueled by wage increases. In 1969 and 1970 annual growth rates were 6.64 and 4.93 respectively. Until 1973, economic growth—maintained largely by government spending—sustained the system of mass production and consumption. However, for many large firms the Accords dramatically increased labor costs. Small firms were not hurt as much because firms with fewer than 50 employees and firms employing temporary workers were exempt from new labor regulations. These exemptions were important because they encouraged many employers to decentralize by subcontracting some production and services to small enterprises and hire more workers on less secure, temporary contracts.

Italy experienced a similar social crisis in the late 1960s, which was followed by labor legislation favorable to workers. Waves of labor conflict began in 1968 and continued into the "Hot Autumn" of 1969, encompassing skilled workers, migrants from southern Italy, women, white-collar workers, and public sector employees. The protestors' demands went beyond the typical union terms of higher wages to challenge the system of production. Strikes in the autumn of 1969 involved a total of 5.5 million workers throughout Italy (Bedani 1995, 150).

Concerned about the effects of continued unrest on political and economic stability, the Italian government and employers held a series of meetings in 1969. The results were employer concessions to most of the unions' demands including a forty-hour week, equal pay increases of a substantial amount for all categories of workers, the right of assembly in the workplace, and the recognition of workers' committees. The final agreement passed by parliament in May 1970 was the Statuto dei Lavoratori.

By the early 1970s, sharp wage increases had completely eliminated the advantages of cheap Italian labor. For example, in 1970 the national wage bill increased by 16.9 percent, and the power of the labor unions meant that wage increases could not easily be stopped. In 1975, the unions were successful in linking wages to price increases through a formal mechanism called the *scala mobile*. Unions also won guarantees for workers who were laid off: such workers would receive up to 80 percent of their wages for a maximum period of twelve months, with employers bearing 8 percent and the government 72 percent of wage costs. Employers' attitudes toward labor unions hardened as profits declined. Employers tried to evade union organization and labor laws by decentralizing production to small enterprises, subcontracting, and moving some production to the underground economy.

In Spain, labor inflexibility was partly an outcome of Franco's labor policies, specifically regulations concerning employment termination and detailed regulations on job classification, contracts, pay structures, and work organization. Many of these regulations survived the Spanish transition to democracy in the mid-1970s. In the mid-to-late 1970s, severe economic recession and the sudden mobilization of unions compounded labor market rigidities. During the transition to democracy, labor unions emerged as a powerful and potentially destabilizing force in Spanish society. When unions were legalized in 1976, the newly formed Comisiones Obreras and the reorganized Unión General de Trabajadores rapidly mobilized. Membership rates sky-rocketed to over 50 percent of the workforce in the late 1970s, only to fall precipitously to less than 15 percent by the early 1980s. Nevertheless, during the transition to democracy the unions gained an important institutional role in economic planning.

Spain's CEOE sees the history of state intervention in the labor market as a severe obstacle to firm profitability and has tried to build a common interest among employers linking free labor markets to antistatism. Employers were successful in increasing labor market flexibility through legislation passed in 1984, which extended the use and variety of temporary contracts. By 1992, temporary contracts covered 32 percent of the working population, compared to an EC average of 9 percent. Since the mid-1980s, temporary contracts have accounted for 90 percent of all employment contracts signed each year (Lucio and Blyton 1995, 350–51).

The failure of mass-based production to sustain economic growth and increasing labor market rigidity forced many employers to pursue more flexible strategies in the 1970s and 1980s. Large firms tried to decentralize production by subcontracting some manufacturing and service jobs to small firms that fell outside labor regulations, or by moving some activities to the underground economy. Economic restructuring also signaled a change in demand for immigrant labor. Large firms no longer required inputs of semi-skilled and unskilled immigrant labor to meet large-scale production requirements. Instead, the new demand for immigrant labor has been concentrated at the margins of the economy in temporary work, in microenterprises, and in the underground economy.

Profitability Squeeze, Restructuring, and Decentralized Demand for Immigrant Labor

The oil crisis of 1973 brought an abrupt end to economic growth in France and a suspension of employment-based immigration, which had been supported by the CNPF. In fact, the CNPF blames its own support of open immigration policies in the 1950s and 1960s for the poor performance of French manufacturing firms after 1973. According to Emmanuel Julien, Director of European and International Affairs for the organization, French firms failed to invest in capital and fell behind technologically because they were dependent on cheap immigrant labor.

Two years after the oil shock of 1973, growth rates in France, Italy, and Spain plummeted (see Figure 7).

Inflexible labor markets, increasing international and intra-European competition, and financial uncertainty caused by exchange rate volatility stung corporate profits. For example, profitability rates plummeted across the G-7 nations in the period between 1965 and 1980, from 17 percent to 11 percent. Manufacturing profitability rates sank from 25 percent to 12 percent (Harrison and Bluestone 1990, 363). To increase profitability, many employers abandoned the model of mass production for more flexible production and employment strategies.

What strategy an employer chose was conditioned by several domestic factors including the strength of labor unions in the firm, government regulations, and available technology and labor resources. In France, the CNPF encouraged employers to have more informal dialogue with employees over wages and working hours, outside the formal employee representation system. The Auroux Laws of 1982, however, sought to curtail this strategy of direct employer-employee communication by requiring regular, compulsory negotiations be-

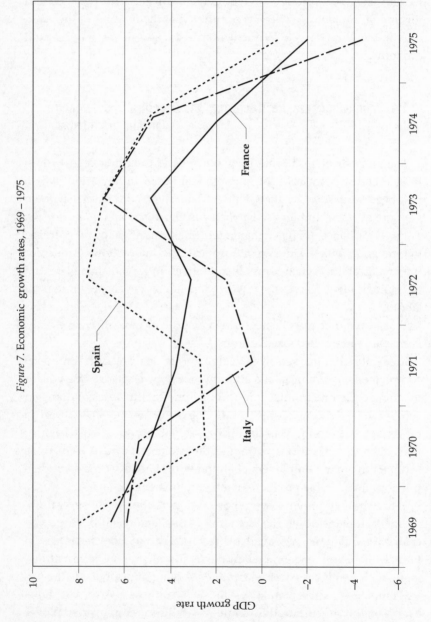

Figure 7. Economic growth rates, 1969 – 1975

Source: ACLP World Political/Economic Database (1995)

tween labor and management. Nonetheless, many employers continued to evade unions and negotiate directly with workers by creating "quality circles" within the firm. Many large firms chose to avoid unions altogether and went outside traditional employment and production systems. High-tech firms competing on the basis of technological skill, for instance, often chose to increase labor flexibility by using nonunionized subcontractors to provide secretarial and other support services, or untraditional temporary and part-time employment contracts that fell outside the purview of unions. In Spain, where temporary contracts are not subject to the same restrictions as permanent contracts, the percentage of the workforce on temporary contracts rose from 15 percent in 1987 to 30 percent in 1991.

In sectors with low technological requirements and high labor-to-capital ratios, such as low-skilled manufacturing, services, and agriculture, the search for profitability often leads to competing on the basis of cheap labor. In these sectors, labor-saving measures, such as part-time and temporary contracts or union avoidance, are more practical and less expensive to implement than capital investments. One consequence of labor-saving strategies has been to amplify labor market dualism between workers in the primary sector, who are protected by unions and government regulations, and those in the secondary sector, who lack the benefits and job security of insiders.

At the same time that large firms have been replacing permanent workers with temporary and part-time employees and subcontracting portions of production, the importance of small and medium sized enterprises (SMEs) to the national economy has increased dramatically. In Italy, national output produced by firms with between twenty and a hundred workers increased from 31 to 34 percent between 1972 and 1980 (Best 1990, 204). In France between 1985 and 1994, the share of manufacturing exports produced by SMEs increased from 22 percent to 29 (OECD 1997c, 101).

In Spain, between 1981 and 1987, the number of mid-sized manufacturing firms grew by 3 percent while the number of large manufacturing firms decreased by the same percentage. During the same period, employment in large Spanish firms decreased by 27 percent. Of the 64,476 manufacturing firms created in Spain between 1980 and 1987, 62,666 had fewer than twenty-five employees and 1,640 had between twenty-five and one hundred employees. The average size of a new firm created during this period in Spain was six employees (OECD 1997c, 231–32).

The industrial restructuring process of the 1970s and 1980s favored the creation and growth of SMEs because of their ability to adjust employment and production with changes in demand. SMEs have an advantage over large firms in that their small, decentralized structure makes it difficult for unions to organize workers and for the government to monitor compliance with labor laws. As a result, SMEs have become a vital part of the economy as subcontractors for large firms, as employment creators, and as contributors to GDP. And government policies have favored the development of SMEs. In France, SMEs employ 69 percent of the workforce and contribute 62 percent of GDP. Italian SMEs officially employ 43 percent of the workforce and contribute 40 percent of GDP. And in Spain, SMEs make up 64 percent of the workforce and 41 percent of GDP (OECD 1997c).

However, the flexibility that has made SMEs profitable has a downside for many workers. In many SMEs, workers have little job security and often receive lower wages and fewer benefits than workers in large firms. For example, in Italy blue-collar workers in large manufacturing firms of over five hundred employees make 16 percent more in wages than workers in firms that employ fewer than twenty (Harrison 1994, 272).

Achievements by employers in numerical and wage flexibility dismantled many of the protections won by labor unions in the 1960s. More important for immigration, flexible specialization has amplified labor market segmentation and increased demand for marginalized workers who are willing to take part-time, temporary, and poorly compensated jobs. The immigrants' precarious legal and economic position meets the needs of employers in the secondary sectors who want flexible workers. Because an immigrant's legal status typically depends on his or her employer guaranteeing a contract, the immigrant can be forced to accept low wages and poor working conditions. Employers enjoy even greater negotiating leverage over illegal immigrants, who need an employment contract to legalize their status and rarely report employer violations to the authorities for fear of deportation.

Tables 2–4 demonstrate the high incidence of immigrants in periph-

Table 2. Immigrant employment in Spain, by sector, 1996

Sector	Number of legal immigrants	Percent of legal immigrants in workforce	Legal immigrants as a percent of total workforce
Agriculture	26,644	16	2
Industry	11,463	6.8	0.4
Construction	14,720	8.8	1
Service	106,081	64	1.2
Other	7,582	4.4	—

Source: Ministry of Labor and Social Affairs (1996b, 1997)

eral sectors of the economy. The clearest example is in personal and domestic services. In Spain, nearly 7 percent of domestic workers are immigrants, and 81 percent of foreign women are domestic workers. Among 424 female immigrant domestic workers surveyed in Madrid and Barcelona in 1990, 10 percent had permanent contracts, another 10 percent had temporary contracts, and 80 percent did not have a written contract (Cachón 1995, 105–24). In France, immigrants make up almost 12 percent of workers in the personal service sectors (Direction de la Population et des Migrations 1995). And in Italy, immigrant workers account for 24 percent of all domestic workers (Economic and Social Research Institute 1997, 7).

In addition to domestic work, immigrants are concentrated in other sectors characterized by a high degree of decentralization, such as construction, agriculture, and hotel and restaurant services.

On the supply side, the number of immigrant workers on the margins of economy has increased as a result of high unemployment among immigrants, family reunification, and illegal immigration. Although immigrant workers in France were the first to be laid off when the economy went sour in the mid-1970s, they did not return home but brought family members to France, who often joined the ranks of the unemployed. In the 1990s, the unemployment rate among non-EU immigrants in France was 33 percent, compared to a national average of 12 percent. Among non-EU immigrants ages 15–24 years the unemployment rate was 53 percent (Direction de la Population et des Migrations 1995).

Weak immigration controls and employment opportunities in the

Table 3. Immigrant employment in Italy, by sector, 1996

Sector	Number of legal immigrants	Percent of legal immigrant workforce	Legal immigrants as percent of total workforce	Number of illegal immigrants	Illegal immigrants as a percent of total irregular employees
Agriculture	28,258	22	6	7,275	7.5
Industry	57,045	44	1	3,283	5.4
Services	43,883	34	0.4	453,551	84.1

Sources: Caritas di Roma (1997); CENSIS (1997)

Table 4. Immigrant employment in France, by sector, 1994

Sector	Number of foreign workers	Percent of foreign workforce	Foreign workers as a percent of total workforce
Agriculture	29,906	2.7	10.8
Industry	234,908	21.7	5.8
Construction	194,624	17.9	17.1
Services	622,357	57.5	4.5

Source: Direction de la Population et des Migrations (1995)

underground economy have attracted illegal immigrants, giving employers an ample supply of cheap immigrant labor. Employers face minimal risks of being sanctioned by the state for hiring illegal immigrants because labor inspectors tend to overlook illegal work that benefits the national economy and helps employers increase labor flexibility.[2]

By shifting demand for immigrant labor to small firms and secondary economic activities, recession and the search for labor flexibility have transformed the immigration preferences of national employers' organizations. Immigrants are no longer crucial to the profitability of large firms, which dominate employers' organizations at the national level. This combined with the politicization of immigration policy, which takes immigration out of the realm of "company" concerns, has discouraged the national employers' organizations from taking an active position on immigration. Although the CNPF still believes that French firms should be able to hire anyone, from any country, who is most qualified for the job, this philosophical position does not translate into an active pro-immigration policy stance. Likewise in Spain, the CEOE argues that most policy discussions relating to immigration have little to do with company concerns. For the CEOE the debate has cen-

[2] Author interviews, Emmanuel Julien, Director of European and International Affairs, CNPF, Paris, 9/9/97; René Moriaux, Research Director, CEVIPOF, Paris, 9/11/97; Walter Actis, Research Director, Colectivo Ioe, Madrid, 10/6/97; Vaifra Palanca, Assistant to Minister Livia Turco, Ministry of Social Solidarity, Rome, 12/5/97; Luigi Trioani, Adviser, Confcomercio, Rome, 12/15/97.

tered overwhelmingly on improving rights for immigrants and border control problems. Also, high native unemployment rates make demands for more immigrant labor contradictory and politically unwise (author interview, Felipe Manzano Sanz, Director of Labor Relations, CEOE, Madrid, November 29, 1996). And, in Italy, Confindustria, Italy's largest employers' association, has not take a position on immigration at the national level because the current Italian legislation on immigration focuses on improving social and political rights for immigrants and police controls.

Despite the ambiguous position of the national employers' associations, some regional and sectoral associations support more open immigration because the firms they represent face labor shortages. As mentioned at the outset of this chapter, agricultural employers in Almería, claimed a shortage of workers and demanded that the quota for 1997, initially set at 1,115, be increased to 5,600. Unión Almeriense de Ganaderos e Agricultores (UAGA), the association that represents local agricultural employers, asked that labor inspections be suspended until the quota was increased because many employers had been forced to hire illegal immigrants. According to the provincial director of the Ministry of Labor for Almería, the UAGA threatened that employers would hire more illegal immigrants because not enough legal ones were available (author interview, José Rodriguez Sanchez, Provincial Director, Ministry of Labor, Almería, November 11, 1997). Ultimately, the quota was increased to 2,180 for 1997, but not with the support of the CEOE.

Similarly, in Italy, only employers' organizations representing small and medium-size firms in northern Italy were interested in the new Italian immigration law of 1998. According to the Ministry of Social Solidarity, Confindustria was not interested in discussion concerning the new law because it represents large firms that employ few immigrant workers. On the other hand, employers' organizations in northern Italy representing small and medium-size firms and artisans, such as Confartigianano, Confcommercio, and Confesercenti, argued that immigrant labor was essential for them to stay competitive. These organizations participated in the policy-making process and committed themselves to further participation by helping determine quotas at the local level (author interview, Vaifra Palanca, Assistant to Minister Livia Turco, Ministry of Social Solidarity, Rome, December 5, 1997).

Conclusion

Since the mid-1970s, increasing firm decentralization has made it difficult for national employers' associations to represent all employers' interests. Therefore, the CNPF, the CEOE, and Confindustria tend to focus on large firm interests, which generally favor a controlled immigration policy because they do not need immigrant labor. Meanwhile, employers who face a shortage of native workers and want access to legal immigrant labor, or employers who want to avoid the high cost and legal complexities of the primary labor market altogether by hiring illegal immigrant labor are free to pursue their individual interests.

Many global and domestic factors were behind the reorganization of the firm in the 1970s and 1980s, most important macroeconomic recession, declining profitability, inflexible labor markets, and complex and costly government labor and tax regulations. For many employers—especially those in areas with low technological requirements, such as domestic service, agriculture, and unskilled manufacturing and construction—the solution to improving profitability was to increase labor flexibility. Consequently, the demand for immigrant labor is now concentrated in the peripheral or secondary economy. Given high unemployment rates, the politicization of immigration policy, and the availability of cheap immigrant labor, the ambivalent position of the national employers' organizations in regard to immigration policy is understandable. At the same time, the pro-immigration position of many individual firms and local and sectoral employers' associations that face labor shortages is also reasonable. Hence, when examining employer preferences about immigration policy one needs to distinguish between official policies of the national employers' associations and what employers do in regions and sectors where immigrant labor is most prevalent.

Because of their ambiguous immigration preferences, French, Italian, and Spanish national employers' associations have refrained from taking an active part in the immigration policy-making process. Instead, labor unions have been the driving force behind efforts to change immigration policy. Nevertheless, immigration policy outcomes are often compatible with employers' interests. In all three countries, the state is incapable of completely controlling immigration and often unwilling to penalize employers who hire illegal immigrants, which gives employers almost risk-free access to illegal immigrant labor. And, in the policy-making process, Italian and Spanish employers have benefited from their tacit alliance with labor union leaders, who have lobbied for more expansive immigration quotas.

5

Patterns of Change in Immigration Policy

similar immigration policy-making pattern has unfolded in Spain, Italy, and France: restrictive laws that place immigrants in a precarious position are followed by reforms that improve their stability. The Stolerú Decrees of 1979, which sought to limit renewals of work and residency permits in France, were succeeded by the creation of a ten-year work and residency permit in 1984. Likewise, in Spain, the 1985 LOE limited most work and residency permits to one year, but in 1996 the work permit system was reformed to allow for more long-term stays. The absence of legal means to immigrate to Italy in the 1980s and early 1990s contributed to the growth of a large illegal immigrant population, which was addressed through amnesties in 1991, 1995, 1998, and 1999.

Several factors help explain this pattern of increasing openness, which I define as policies that open avenues for legal immigration and increase the stability of legal and illegal immigrant workers. The most important relationship is between labor union action and the immigration policy-making process. The ascendancy of labor unions in the policy-making process is a crucial factor in immigration policy reform. Labor unions participate in the policy-making process through formal contacts in institutional settings, informal contacts with government officials, and public protest.

Employers sometimes support labor unions' efforts to raise immigration quotas, but more often employers are publicly silent on immigration issues. According to one Italian employer representative, the current immigration situation favors small-and medium-size employers who have easy access to illegal immigrant labor, yet little risk of being caught and fined. As a result, there is little incentive for employers take a public position on immigration (author interview, Luigi Trioani, adviser, Confcomercio, Rome, December 15, 1997). Other employer representatives cite the political nature of immigration as a reason for not taking an active part in the policy-making process. According to a Spanish employer representative, immigration policy discussions held among labor unions, immigrant associations, government officials, and employers in the Forum for the Integration of Immigrants have little to do with "company" concerns (author interview, Felipe Manzano Sanz, Director of Labor Relations, CEOE, Madrid, October 9, 1997). In addition, high unemployment rates in Spain, Italy, and France have discouraged employers from taking a politically unpopular stance in favor of immigration. Finally, the decentralization and diversity of company interests make it difficult for a national employers' organization to formulate a comprehensive position on immigration. For these reasons, European employers have not been a major player in the immigration policy-making process since the early 1970s. Nonetheless, by virtue of their silence they are tacitly allied with labor unions as proponents of open immigration policies, and their support has helped create more legal avenues for immigration to Spain, Italy, and France.

Isolating Labor's Influence in the Immigration Policy-Making Process

Isolating the effects of labor union activities on immigration policy is problematic because immigration is a complex issue that affects many groups. For example, unions often act with the support of immigrant associations in their efforts to achieve more moderate immigration policies. However, these groups sometimes compete for access to policy-makers. For example, some Italian labor leaders were disgruntled because policy-makers consulted with immigrant associations more than with unions about the 1998 Italian immigration bill. On the other side of the debate, anti-immigrant groups, such as the National Front in France and the Northern League in Italy, see immigrants as a social and economic threat. These groups favor restrictive immigration policies and oppose the efforts of labor unions to increase quotas, legalize illegal immigrants, and facilitate family reunification.

My focus here is on the labor market aspects of immigration policy, in which unions display their clearest influence, and that of other groups is minimized.

In addition to group influence, institutional, political, and economic factors complicate the policy-making process. For example, labor's ability to influence immigration policy often depends on what political party has the majority in government. When leftist parties control government, labor leaders enjoy greater access to the policy-making process and can make positive policy contributions. When the government majority is conservative, labor leaders often are excluded from the policy-making process because conservative parties do not need labor's support for electoral success. In these cases, labor exercises its influence through protest, and may have veto power over restrictive legislation. In France, where power has been shared between the left and the right during periods of "cohabitation," labor's influence has been weaker when the prime minister is from the right, since the prime minister typically controls the domestic agenda.

How Changes in Government Affect Labor's Ability to Influence Policy

The party-union link is an important relationship in the immigration policy-making process, especially in France where changes in government precede changes in immigration policy. After the suspension of immigration to France in 1974, conservative governments have cracked down on illegal immigration and restricted work permit renewals and family reunification despite protest from labor unions. Even when power was shared between socialist President Mitterrand and a conservative majority in parliament, from 1986 to 1988 and 1992 to 1993, conservative governments restricted immigration. On the other hand,

when the socialists have enjoyed the majority in parliament, some restrictive immigration policies have been reversed, and many illegal immigrants have been allowed to legalize their status. For example, the
1998 Chevènement Law reversed some aspects of the restrictive Pasqua
and Debré laws passed in 1993 and 1997 respectively. And, in 1981, the
newly elected socialist government followed through on its promise to
grant amnesty to thousands of illegal immigrants.

However, the correlation between conservative governments and restrictive immigration policies does not always hold. Frequently, when
conservative governments exclude labor unions from the policy-making process, unions use protest to veto restrictive policy outcomes. For
instance, Italian labor leaders are more prone to organize public protest
against conservative governments, in part because they are excluded
from formal procedures, but also because there is little political risk involved (author interview, Adriana Buffardi, President, IRES-CGIL,
Rome, December 16, 1997). The Italian unions were quick to organize a
large protest against the restrictive aspects of the proposed Dini Decree
in 1995. The center-right Dini government excluded the unions from
any formal or informal discussions concerning the decree, leaving the
unions with little recourse other than public demonstration. The union
protest convinced socialist members of parliament to vote against the
decree and pass a more moderate version that included an amnesty.

Socialist governments are more likely to consult with unions during
the policy-making process because they rely on labor support for electoral and political success. As participants in the process labor unions
can make positive policy inputs. Spanish labor leaders were consulted
regularly by the Gonzalez government during the 1996 reform process,
and the Italian unions were involved in the 1991 reform. During the
1997–1998 reform process, however, Italian unions were reluctant to
protest against what they viewed as restrictive aspects of the proposed
immigration reform; they did not want to threaten the precarious majority held by the socialists or damage relations with Livia Turco, who
coauthored the law and headed the Ministry of Social Solidarity.[1] As a

---

[1] Author interviews, Aly Baba Faye, former Director, Coordinamento Immigrati,
CGIL, Rome, 12/1/97, Adriana Buffardi, President, IRES-CGIL, Rome, 12/16/97, and
Angelo Masetti, National Representative for Migration, UIL, Rome, 12/3/97.

result, labor achieved many, but not all, of its policy goals through formal and informal government consultations.

Shifting Institutional Control of the Immigration Policy-Making Process

Over the past twenty-five years, recession and unemployment in France have helped transform the public perception of immigration from an economic advantage to a security risk. One consequence of this "securitization" of immigration has been that control over the policy-making process has been transferred from the Ministry of Labor, where labor unions usually enjoy long-term institutional contacts, to the Ministry of the Interior, where unions have little experience. As a result, labor leaders have lost some influence over policy outcomes.

While labor officials in all three countries are primarily concerned with the supply and demand for immigrant workers, interior officials focus on policing, law and order, prisons, drug trafficking, and terrorism. The increasing authority of the Interior Ministry is evident at the local, national, and intergovernmental levels. For example, permit renewals in Spain, Italy, and France are solely the domain of the local police, who represent the Ministry of the Interior, though until recently, these renewals were handled jointly by the Ministries of Labor and Interior in Spain and Italy. Not surprisingly, labor leaders are concerned that this transfer of authority will threaten the employment security of immigrants, since the police are not concerned with the labor aspects of immigration. Hence, labor leaders are demanding a continued role for the Ministry of Labor at the local level (CCOO 1997a).

At the national level, evidence of this institutional shift is most apparent in France, where the Ministry of the Interior, under the leadership of Charles Pasqua, clamped down on immigration in 1986–1988 and 1992–1996. Pasqua increased police powers to detain and expel illegal immigrants and created a new government office under the Ministry of the Interior, the Office Central pour la Répression de l'Immigration Irrégulière et de l'Emploi sans Titres (OCRIEST), to monitor and control the employment of illegal immigrants. The institutional transfer of administrative control and policy initiative to the Ministry of the

Interior is the most important constraint on labor's ability to influence immigration policy.

At the European level, intergovernmental institutions have dominated efforts to coordinate immigration policy, to the detriment of Community institutions such as the European Commission and European Parliament. Intergovernmental institutions such as the Schengen Group, the Trevi Group, and the Ad Hoc Immigration Group usually consist of interior ministers who approach immigration as a security issue. The mandate of the Trevi Group, for instance, includes internal security, international crime, drug trafficking and the policing of borders. Likewise, the Schengen Agreements include common policies on external border control, such as visas, and measures to control criminals and terrorists. The Schengen Agreements are backed by a computerized information system that provides data to the police on asylum seekers and immigrants who have been refused entry into another member state.

Although most labor leaders favor a coherent European immigration policy, they are concerned about the transfer of authority to the European level, given the track record of intergovernmental institutions. For example, labor unions want all workers, including legal immigrants, to have the right to move freely within the European Union. However, the free movement of legal immigrants for employment purposes is restricted among the European Union member states. Labor unions and employers may gain more influence over immigration decisions at the European level as a result of the 1997 Amsterdam Treaty, which promises to open the policy-making process by improving transparency and increasing the role of the European Parliament and Commission. Nevertheless, wresting control over immigration from member states will be a difficult and long-term project for Community institutions.

Why Poor Macroeconomic Performance Does Not Necessarily Signal Restrictions

The oil crisis of 1973 and the recession that followed are common explanations for the crackdown on immigration to France in 1974.

French policy-makers, employers, and some labor leaders adopted an economic rationale that a temporary ban on employment-based immigration would help abate economic crisis and rising unemployment levels. Applying this same logic, one would expect economic growth and a tight labor market to be accompanied by more open immigration policies, as was the case in France from 1960 to 1973, when the average annual growth rate was 4.59 and unemployment around 2 percent.

Yet although French economic performance and immigration policy appeared to be positively correlated during the 1960s and 1970s, the state of the economy does not explain the recent moderation in immigration policy that has occurred in Spain, Italy, and France. In the 1990s, increased quotas for immigrant workers, amnesties, and long-term work and residency permits accompanied high unemployment rates and slow growth. In Italy and France the average annual unemployment rate in 1990–1996 was nearly 12 percent, and in Spain over 20 percent. Growth rates were also slow during this period, with an average annual growth rate of 1.8 percent in Spain, 1.4 percent in France, and 1.3 percent in Italy.

Therefore, to understand the relationship between economic performance and immigration policy in the 1990s, one must examine the labor demands of specific sectors and firms in highly segmented markets, rather than evaluating economic performance on a macrolevel. Employment-based quotas are increasing despite high native unemployment rates because of labor shortages in specific sectors such as agriculture and construction. For example, in September 1999, Spain signed an agreement with Morocco that allows 300,000 temporary migrants per year to work in Spain's agriculture and construction sectors.

Labor leaders also maintain their objective of unifying the primary and secondary labor markets by moderating immigration policy. Labor leaders have lobbied the government to legalize illegal immigrants, amplify immigration quotas, and extend work and residency permits because they see an entrenched demand for precarious immigrant workers in the secondary labor market. Because of labor market segmentation there is no one-to-one relationship between economic performance and immigration policy.

How Labor Union Actions Help Change Immigration Policy

According to representatives of labor unions, three main avenues exist for expressing their policy interests: formal, institutional contacts with government officials; informal contacts with government officials; and protest.

Formal, institutional contacts include meetings with government officials, business leaders, and other interested groups to discuss immigration policy. Through formal contacts labor leaders may make positive policy inputs. More often, however, this forum is reserved for information exchanges between government officials and interest groups. Hence, most labor leaders find these meetings the least effective means to influence policy.

According to labor leaders, informal contacts such as private meetings, phone calls, and letters to government officials are much more effective than formal meetings. In informal contacts, labor leaders' long-term, institutional links with the Ministry of Labor give them a privileged position in the policy-making process compared to most nongovernmental organizations and immigrant associations.

Some leaders believe public protest is an effective means for vetoing restrictive outcomes. The French CGT, Italian CGIL and Spanish CCOO have used protest as an alternative to formal and informal consultations when excluded from the policy-making process. However, some labor leaders warn that protest will fail to impress policy-makers if support for immigration is weak or divided within the union.

Formal Contacts

In Spain, Italy, and France, institutional settings to discuss immigration policy among government officials and interest groups abound. However, most labor leaders believe formal institutional settings are the least effective way to influence policy because unions play only a consultory role.

In France, labor unions and employers can participate in meetings of the Office des Migrations Internationales (OMI), where technicalities of immigration law are discussed. Labor unions, employers associations, immigrant associations, and government officials participate in meet-

ings of the Conseil National pour l'Intégration des Populations Immi-
grées (CNIPI), which conducts research, presents proposals, and sometimes offers its opinions on government proposals. Labor unions are
also involved with the Human Rights Commission, which works on issues related to immigrants' rights. Although the Commission does not
specialize in immigration, it receives considerable press coverage, making it a powerful voice on the issue. Finally, labor unions have some influence over how funds are allocated by a government agency called
Fond d'Action Sociale (FAS). FAS finances programs to help immigrants integrate into French society, and these programs are carried out
by labor unions and immigrant associations.

French unions have varying levels of influence in these institutions.
For example, in OMI meetings labor leaders find they can sometimes
achieve minor changes in the finer points of immigration law. Unions
are one of many groups represented in the Human Rights Commission,
but union influence is diluted by the numerous interest groups involved in the Commission, which include nongovernmental associations, researchers, religious organizations, ministry officials, and members of the National Assembly and Senate (author interview, Bruno
Quemada, Representative for Immigration, FO, Paris, September 9,
1997).

In Italy, immigration policy is discussed among government officials,
labor unions, and employers in the National Council for Immigration,
the Commission for Immigration Flows, and the National Council for
the Economy and Work (CNEL). The National Council for Immigration
consists of labor unions, immigrant associations, nongovernmental
organizations, and government officials. The Council reports to the
Ministry of Labor. The Commission for Immigration Flows includes
labor unions, employer representatives, and government officials. It
has met annually since 1991 to discuss quotas. Although it now reports
to the Ministry of Foreign Affairs, this committee has been reorganized
under the 1998 Italian Immigration Law as a result of the new quota
policy. The CNEL deals with all labor issues, including immigrant
labor.

The corporatist structure of Italian politics as exemplified by the
CNEL, which represents both business and labor, mandates that employers and labor unions are consulted in the policy-making process.

However, as in the French case, these institutions are purely consultory. According to one union leader, in the case of immigration policy, Italy lacks a strong formal, institutional structure, and the government does not take seriously the proposals of institutions such as the National Council for Immigration (author interview, Aly Baba Faye, former Director, Coordinamento Immigrati, CGIL, Rome, December 1, 1997).

In Spain, the main arena for discussing immigration policy is the Forum for the Integration of Immigrants, which was created in 1995. Labor unions, employers, and nongovernmental organizations are represented at Forum meetings. Labor ministry officials regularly attend meetings, and in 1997 officials from the Ministry of the Exterior and Ministry of the Interior began attending. The purpose of Forum meetings is for government officials to share information with interested groups and for unions, immigrant associations, and employers to express their opinions. According to a representative from the Ministry of the Interior, however, unions and nongovernment organizations often fail to understand that the government does not have to follow proposals made by the Forum.

The Forum has been unable to influence policy because it lacks the resources—both human and financial—to make valuable proposals. As a result, the government often turns to independent consultants when it wants proposals on immigration policy. The regular functioning of the Forum, which was initially established to meet two to three times per year, was stymied by the change in government in 1996. Created by the socialist Gonzalez government in 1995, the Forum had met only once to discuss substantive issues before the Partido Popular won the 1996 elections. Since Jose Maria Aznar took office, the Forum has met irregularly because, according to labor leaders, the Partido Popular is not interested in immigration.

In sum, French, Italian, and Spanish labor leaders do not see formal institutions as an effective way to influence policy because the purpose of these institutions is solely for government officials to consult with interest groups. Consultation can take place before or after policy is made, and frequently occurs after the fact. Hence, these institutions can serve as a means for government officials simply to inform labor leaders and employers of government decisions. Formal, institutional settings are also seen as ineffective because most interest groups lack sufficient human and financial resources to devote much energy to their efficient functioning. Nevertheless, labor unions continue to participate in formal institutional settings because they provide a regular source of dialogue with policy-makers.

Informal Contacts

Informal contacts with government officials, which may include private meetings, phone calls, and letters, are a more personal and direct way to influence policy. However, the effectiveness of informal contacts often depends on a socialist majority willing to give labor access, as well as the Ministry of Labor's involvement, in the policy-making process. For example, in shaping the 1998 Italian immigration law, the unions first used their contacts with ministry officials to make the new quota policy open to all potential immigrants. When the bill was sent to parliament, labor leaders contacted members of parliament to press for amendments that the government had not approved, such as a shortened waiting period for permanent residency. In both cases the unions used informal contacts successfully to get their proposals included in the new law (author interview, Vaifra Palanca, Assistant to Minister Livia Turco, Ministry of Social Solidarity, Rome, December 5, 1997).

In 1995, the Spanish unions, with the support of several immigrant associations and nongovernment organizations, petitioned Prime Minister Gonzalez through a series of letters and proposals for meetings to discuss immigration reform. The meetings were granted, and on January 30, 1996, Francisco Soriano, Director of Migration for the CCOO, wrote to the prime minister that although not all the expectations of the unions were met, he believed that the proposals made in the meeting responded to many of the needs of immigrants. However, Soriano also expressed his concern that the proposals had not yet formally been made into law (CCOO 1996a). On January 31, 1996, *El Pais* published an article about the letter sent by Soriano, and another letter sent by a representative of the UGT, to President and Prime Minister Gonzalez. The article cites a promise by Gonzalez to the unions to approve the proposals in 1995 (*El Pais* 1996). On February 2, 1996, the proposals were made into a Real Decreto (Royal Decree).

Formal meetings on an annual, quarterly, or ad hoc basis do not allow for continuous contact with ministry officials. This is a problem in Italy, where labor leaders believe the fluid nature of politics requires ongoing discussions with ministry officials if labor leaders want to play a role in the policy-making process. For example, between August and December of 1990, the unions held frequent and successful informal meetings with ministry officials to discuss the Martelli immigration bill. However, the frequency of informal contacts with government officials depends on how much the government needs the support of unions. Government leaders of the right and center, such as Dini and Silvio Berlusconi, were much less dependent on labor's support than the socialist Martelli.

Finally, most labor leaders from the French CFDT and FO believe that when support for immigration among union affiliates is weak and divided, informal contacts are more effective than formal contacts or public protest.

Protests

Labor unions have used protest to force conservative governments to rescind restrictive policy proposals. In the late 1980s and early 1990s, the Italian and Spanish unions organized mass demonstrations to heighten government awareness of illegal immigration and gain access to the policy-making process. For example, in 1989, the unions led one of the largest and most successful protests of Italian immigration policy after the murder of a South African immigrant near Naples. According to Aly Baba Faye, former Director of CGIL's Coordinamento Immigrati, this protest was the impetus for a thorough reform of Italian immigration law in 1991. About 200,000 people participated in the Rome protest, with the unions providing transportation for thousands of protestors who came from other cities. The protestors demanded a reform of the 1986 immigration law, a regularization of illegal immigrants, and an active role in the policy-making process. For the first time, the Italian government worked closely with labor unions in designing the new immigration law, which legalized thousands of illegal immigrants and created procedures for legal immigration.

In the 1970s, the French unions, with the support of immigrant associations, effectively used protest to veto rent increases imposed by conservative governments in dormitories managed by the government controlled Sonacotra housing agency. In 1979, French unions were also active in demonstrating against the Stolerú Decrees that limited renewals of work and residency permits and the Barre-Bonnet Law that facilitated deportation of illegal immigrants. The socialist government elected in 1980 reacted to labor's demands by reversing many of these restrictive policies imposed by conservative majorities.

Although protest can be effective in vetoing restrictive policy outcomes, it can also be dangerous. If the union does not have sufficient internal support, protest may make the union appear weak and thus diminish the importance of an issue (author interview, François Srocynski, Representative for Immigration, CFDT, Paris, September 17, 1997). Likewise the FO, which represents mainly white-collar workers, avoids public protest on immigration because it believes that the issue is too divisive (author interview, Bruno Quemada, Representative for Immigration, FO, Paris, September 22, 1997).

On the other hand, the CGT, a more blue-collar union, believes that mobilization adds to the workers' understanding of immigration issues. According to CGT leadership, protest must happen simultaneously with government consultations to influence policy effectively (author interview, Gérard Chemouil, Representative for Immigration, CGT, Paris, September 18, 1997). For example, when the most recent French immigration law was being discussed in the fall of 1997, the CGT mounted protests against aspects of the bill prior to the meeting of the Human Rights Commission. The CGT felt it could not wait for the Commission to give its opinion, but had to act first to show its disapproval of the restrictive aspects of the proposed legislation.

Patterns of Change and Evidence of Labor's Influence

Several cases of change in immigration policy demonstrate how unions have used formal contacts, informal contacts, and protest to achieve many of their policy goals. In Spain, the unions engaged in protracted campaigns that involved formal institutional meetings, informal contacts, and protest. Spanish labor leaders' efforts to reform the 1985 LOE did not gain momentum until the early 1990s, and it was ten years before the LOE was modified. Over time, labor gained increasing access to the policy-making process through activism on the national and local levels. And in the end, union input was critical to the reform process.

The French cases are more complex and involve many political actors, so the influence of the unions is less clear. The unions provided an institutional avenue for immigrants to express their concerns to policy-makers, and in the 1970s won several reforms that increased immigrants' rights in the workplace. But although the unions were an important voice for moderation, it was the election of a socialist government that stimulated immigration reform in 1981. Likewise, the 1997–1998 immigration reform process got underway with the election of a socialist majority in 1996. Although the CGT was active in protesting the restrictive Pasqua Laws and the CGT, CFDT, and FO mounted campaigns to fight racism and discrimination in the workplace, their direct influence in the reform process was minimal.

In two of the Italian cases, labor unions took full advantage of their institutional access to the policy-making process to achieve many of their goals and used protest successfully to directly affect the policy-making process. In 1989, union protests forced immigration to the top of the government's agenda and gave the unions direct access to the policy-making process. And in 1996, union protests coerced the Dini government into reconsidering a decree that would have granted more discretion to the police. But in 1997 the unions refrained from protesting what they saw as restrictive aspects of the new immigration bill because they did not want to jeopardize relations with the government. Many labor leaders conclude that unions failed to block restrictive measures, such as increasing police discretion over deportation, because they were unwilling to use protest.

Spanish Unions: A Leading Voice for Reform. In February 1996, the Spanish government passed an immigration reform that, in the law's own words, "represented the culmination of a long period of consultations and negotiations with labor unions, nongovernmental organizations and immigrant associations" (Boletin Oficial de las Cortes Generales 1996). The reform met the labor unions' goals in three ways.

- A new system of long-term work and residency permits replaced annual renewals. Immigrants could apply for a two-year permit after residing legally in Spain for just one year. The two-year permit could be renewed for three years, and after six years an immigrant could obtain permanent residency.

- Restrictions on family reunification were lifted.
- A four-month period for undocumented immigrants to apply for amnesty was established.

In the early 1990s, Spanish labor unions gradually mounted a campaign to moderate the 1985 LOE, which labor leaders saw as the cause of immigrants' precarious situations. The LOE restricted legal immigration, and the growing population of illegal immigrants had little opportunity to legalize their status. Hence, labor leaders wanted an amnesty that would bring illegal immigrant workers out of the underground economy.

Compounding the number of clandestine entries were undocumented immigrants who were unable to renew their permits. Under the LOE, permit renewals were difficult and costly because immigrants had to return to their country of origin to obtain a new visa. Because of bureaucratic inefficiencies, many immigrants with one-year permits were prone to long periods of institutionalized illegality. Labor leaders wanted a clarification of the renewal process and longer-term permits, including permanent residency.

The ambiguity of Spain's family reunification policy and restrictions placed on immigrant families from North Africa and the Philippines made family reunification virtually impossible for most immigrants between 1985 and 1996. Restrictions on family reunification contributed to immigrant instability by forcing immigrants to live without their families or to live with their families in a semi-clandestine status. The unions wanted a reform that would allow family reunification without restrictions and that would grant family members the right to work.

The Spanish unions pursued a multipronged approach in their efforts to reform the LOE. The first task was to put immigration reform on the socialist government's agenda, and then to gain institutional access to the policy-making process. Led by the CCOO, the unions and immigrant associations organized local and national protests to raise awareness about the precarious situation of immigrants, which culminated in a nationwide protest on November 27, 1994. The protests received nationwide media coverage, with close to 15,000 participants in Barcelona and thousands more in other Spanish cities.

In addition to public protest, union leaders used their long-term contacts in the Ministry of Labor to pressure government officials. The unions also submitted various proposals and petitions aimed at reforming the LOE. As a result, the socialist government granted the unions increasing access to the policy-making process and funds for immigrant programs. It created institutions for policy-makers to discuss and research immigration with input from the unions, nongovernmental organizations, employers, academics, and immigrant associations, such as the Forum for the Integration of Immigrants. At the local level, government funding helped the unions improve and expand immigrant outreach programs through the CITE (CCOO) and Centro Guia (UGT) offices. One of primary functions of these offices was, and is, to help immigrants navigate the complex legal process of permit renewals and legalization.

Through their actions at the local and national levels, the unions helped reveal inconsistencies in the LOE that had created a growing illegal immigrant population in Spain. Recognizing that the unions had expertise in immigration issues, President and Prime Minister Gonzalez promised that any reform of the current immigration law would include input from unions and nongovernmental organizations (author interview, Victor Gomez, immigration lawyer, CCOO, Madrid, October 29, 1997). In 1995, the socialist government held an immigration conference in which unions played a leading role and made positive policy inputs.

The unions faced little organized opposition to moderating immigration policy. In fact, Spanish public opinion polls from 1996 show that only 5.4 percent of Spaniards were concerned about immigration from less-developed countries and only 8.3 percent believed Spanish immigration law was too lenient (Centro de Investigaciónes Sociológicas 1996). The cumulative effect of protests, informal contacts, and participation in formal institutional settings helped the unions achieve many of their goals in the 1996 immigration reform.

French Unions: The Move to Protect Immigrants. In the 1970s, the CGT and CFDT became increasingly important channels for voicing immigrants' interests to the state. For example, French unions gained workplace rights for immigrants in 1972 and 1974. The CGT and CFDT also protested against proposals by the conservative Chirac and Barre governments to restrict work permit renewals and increase police powers to deport immigrants. In the early 1980s, the new socialist government reversed many restrictive measures. Immigration policy reforms included an amnesty, the creation of a ten-year permit, protection against deportation without due process, and more liberal family reunification. These reforms met most of the goals of the unions, who helped shape the debate by providing a channel for immigrants' concerns to be heard by policy-makers.

According to one French immigration expert, the events of May 1968 were a prerequisite for cooperation between immigrant workers and unions in the 1970s. The participation of immigrants in the social unrest of 1968 caused labor leaders to realize that immigrants were an important group of workers who were becoming increasingly vocal (author interview, Michel Cansot, Chief of Service, OMI, Paris, September 10, 1997). Despite the difficulties of reconciling the specific needs of immigrant workers with the unions' broad-based strategies, unions and immigrant workers found themselves to be interdependent. Unions provided the institutional framework for immigrant workers to channel their demands to policy-makers. And militant immigrant workers gave a second wind to unions, which were rapidly losing strength because of economic recession, increasing unemployment rates, and economic austerity measures.

The Sonacotra housing strikes of 1973–1980 exemplify the unique problems faced by immigrants and illustrate how unions provided institutional legitimacy for immigrants to voice their demands. In 1973, immigrant workers initiated housing strikes to protest rent increases and poor living conditions in worker dormitories controlled by the Sonacotra housing authority. In 1975, the CGT led the first effort to coordinate the demands of immigrants living in different dormitories. Soon after, the more radical immigrant-led Coordinating Committee emerged, which better represented immigrant interests. However, the Coordinating Committee did not replace the CGT in negotiations because the Sonacotra housing authority refused to negotiate with them.

In 1975, the CGT and Sonacotra signed an agreement that was denounced by the rival Coordinating Committee. The agreement did not hold, and immigrant strike activity increased in 1976. The government reacted by issuing deportation orders to many of the strikers, a move that was denounced by the CGT and CFDT. The strike was eventually settled in the early 1980s with the government agreeing to improve housing conditions.

Ultimately, the competition between the Coordinating Committee and the CGT forced the immigrants to realize they needed unions to make their demands effectively. The competition also sensitized unions to the needs of immigrants. So, ultimately, the housing strike helped institutionalize immigrant representation in French unions (Schain 1994). The CGT and CFDT also led other militant actions by immigrant workers in the late 1970s. Examples include the Paris Metro cleaners' strike of 1977, the Malvilles nuclear generator strike of 1979, and the Lorraine mines strike of 1980 (Ireland 1994).

The socialist government elected in 1981 reacted to union demands made on behalf of immigrants during the late 1970s, and quickly implemented several reforms to improve the security of legal and illegal immigrants. The government suspended the expulsion of illegal immigrants and reaffirmed the right to family reunification. It also set in motion a reform of work and residency permits, which included the creation of a ten-year residency permit. In addition, between 1981 and 1983, the government legalized more than 140,000 illegal immigrants.

By acting as a conduit for expressing immigrant interests to policymakers, unions helped pave the way for immigration reform. French unions effectively used protest to heighten awareness of immigrants' precarious situations caused by restrictive immigration policies. However, the necessary condition for a moderation in French immigration policy was the election of the socialist majority that shared union concerns about restrictive immigration policies.

Socialists and the 1998 French Immigration Reform. The French immigration reform of 1998 was also accompanied by union activity on behalf of immigrant workers and the election of a socialist majority in parliament.

The reform of French immigration policy in the early 1980s was short-lived. Immigration was a focal point of the 1986 legislative elections, as the electorate reacted to the combined effects of socialist policies on immigration, high unemployment rates, and the anti-immigrant discourse of the National Front (FN), which enjoyed its first major political breakthrough. Mainstream conservatives, fearful of losing votes to far-right FN candidates, adopted many of the FN's xenophobic positions. The conservatives regained the majority in parliament, ushering in a period of cohabitation with socialist President Mitterrand.

Since the mid-1980s, public debate on immigration has become increasingly polarized, leaving little common ground for moderate policies. From 1986 to 1988, the conservative majority, led by Prime Minister Jacques Chirac, emphasized the security and control aspects of immigration and increased police powers to deport immigrants believed to be a threat to public order. During a second period of cohabitation in 1992–1993, Interior Minister Pasqua further tightened immigration controls and limited the social and civil rights of immigrants.

Although French unions opposed this shift, they took little action. One French immigration authority argues that since their successes in the 1970s, unions have faced three obstacles in their ability to influence immigration policy. First, the drop in union membership has severely undercut labor's political power. Second, the importance of labor immigration has declined. Third, the labor market has changed so that immigrants now fill the most precarious jobs, which are not covered by the unions (author interview, Marie Thérèse Join Lambert, Inspector General, Department of Social Affairs, Paris, September 22, 1997).

In addition, immigrants gained the right to form their own associations in 1981. Although unions and immigrant associations share many of the same goals, the growth of immigrant associations has detracted from union strength. For example, many second-generation immigrants, who were unemployed or employed in the underground economy, may have been more attracted to membership in immigrant associations than labor unions. And unions faced growing opposition to immigration within their own ranks, as members felt the effects of economic recession and rising unemployment. The unions found it difficult to convince French workers to support immigration when many union members were in a precarious employment situation themselves, and were thus sympathetic to the anti-immigrant rhetoric of the National Front (author interview, François Srocynski, Representative for Immigration, CFDT, Paris, 9/17/97).

To challenge the Pasqua Laws effectively, the unions had to find a way to connect the interests of immigrant workers with those of French workers. They did this by focusing on workplace racism and discrimination, problems faced by women, young people, and long-term unemployed, the underground economy, and immigrants. In 1995 and 1996, the FO conducted a study of racism in the workplace among FO militants in Paris and Yvelines. The study revealed that racism in the workplace is a problem, and that efforts to end it must be continuous and locally driven. Likewise, the CFDT did a four-year study of workplace racism that ended in 1997. Now CFDT leaders are trying to follow up on that study by educating local militants and workers about racism and discrimination. The research arm of the CGT has also conducted several studies of racism in the workplace. One that focused on discrimination in the public transportation sector examined why so few cases of discrimination are actually reported.

In 1997, the socialists regained the majority in parliament. One of their first moves was to call for a reform of the Pasqua Laws and to commission reports on immigration and nationality. The report on immigration took a market-oriented approach that recognized the inevitability of migration while trying to establish a rational policy that would take immigration out of a heated public debate. The authors sought to put a barrier between legal and illegal immigration by further limiting the latter while easing controls on the former. For example, the report proposed to curtail administrative controls over family reunification and student visas. At the same time, it proposed to attack the labor market demand for illegal immigration and enforce deportations of illegal immigrants. While the report was being prepared, over 300 meetings were conducted with local actors, such as police, labor union militants, and nongovernmental organizations (author interview, Patrick Weil, Director, CNRS, Paris, September 26, 1997).

In the fall of 1997, the immigration report was opened to parliamentary debate. The unions participated in the debate through formal meetings of the Human Rights Commission, which gave its opinion on the immigration reform bill in October. Also, the CFDT and CGT took part in public protests calling for the legalization of the *sans-papiers* and a repeal of the Pasqua Laws. In these protests, the leadership of the CGT and CFDT demanded the following: a more liberal family reunification policy; a return of immigrants who were deported without due process; dissolution of OCRIEST; a moratorium on expulsions; restoration of social welfare programs for immigrants; and better access to permanent residency.

Nonetheless, many labor leaders were not satisfied with the outcome of the reform process because the socialists did not go far enough in repealing the Pasqua Laws. The influence of unions was minimal because the reform process was driven by the desire to find a consensus position between the moderate factions of the left and right. But the unions did achieve some of their policy goals, including an amnesty for the *sans-papiers* and a more liberal family reunification policy.

The CGT was by far the most active of the three main unions in pushing for reform of the Pasqua Laws. In 1996, immigration was the central theme of the CGT's 8th National Conference. Also in 1996, the CGT sent President Chirac a petition signed by 25,000 people calling for the repeal of the Pasqua Laws.

In 1997, the CGT conducted a highly publicized nationwide campaign against racism in the workplace. Named the *Tour de France*, it was an effort to educate and inform the union's members, other workers, and local authorities about the problems of racism. Over a four-month period the campaign visited several cities in France, including several National Front strongholds. In all, 8,480 people participated in CGT meetings. As part of this campaign, the CGT aired two television advertisements that focused on racism in the workplace, and these ads reached an estimated 8.5 million people. Finally, press coverage of the campaign was nationwide and coincided with the 1997 immigration reform process.

Unions, especially the CGT and CFDT, have remained active in the immigration debate through protests on behalf of the *sans-papiers*, conducting research on racism and discrimination, and participating in formal institutional settings. However, unlike Spanish, French union activity on behalf of immigrants is challenged by an organized anti-immigrant opposition, which has heavily influenced conservative rhetoric. Hence, without the election of a socialist majority committed to immigration reform, the 1998 law would not have been possible.

Italian Unions: Putting Immigration on the Government Agenda. In 1989, Italian labor unions staged perhaps the most effective use of public protest to influence immigration reform. Officially, protesters were reacting to the murder of a South African immigrant by Italian youths outside of Naples. But more generally the unions that organized the protest and provided transportation to Rome for thousands of Italians wanted a more comprehensive immigration law that would address the problems of clandestine immigration and immigrant exploitation by promoting legal immigration and by legalizing illegal immigrants in Italy. Some 200,000 people participated in the protest, which became the largest on behalf of immigrants.

Italian labor unions saw the 1986 immigration law as only a partial attempt at reform. The Italian economic miracle of the 1970s and 1980s caused labor shortages, especially in northern Italy. Initially, the government tried to encourage internal migration from the south to fill these vacancies. But when these attempts failed, Italy turned to immigrant labor through the 1986 law. According to one prominent labor leader, in the mid-1980s both employers and unions wanted an immigration policy that would attract immigrant workers to Italy (author interview, Aly Baba Faye, former Director, Coordinamento Immigrati, CGIL, Rome, December 1, 1997). However, the 1986 law failed in its attempt to apply a quota system to control entries according to labor market needs. Instead, the old system of ad hoc administrative decrees continued to determine the entry and stay of immigrants. Consequently, labor leaders believed a more comprehensive policy was necessary.

In writing the new legislation, Italian labor leaders worked directly with Claudio Martelli, the socialist vice president of the Council of Ministers, which is the second highest post in government. According to a representative of the UIL, union participation in these meetings was a direct result of the September protest, which forced Martelli to seek the support of unions and put immigration reform on the top of his agenda (author interview, Angelo Masetti, National Representative for Migration UIL, Rome, December 3, 1997).

Interestingly, Italy's extreme right political parties, the Northern League and the Movimento Socialista Italiano (MSI), did not mount strong parliamentary opposition to the Martelli bill, which met with widespread but not unanimous support in government. Instead, the strongest opposition came from members of the Partito Repubblicano

Italiano (PRI), who were part of the governing coalition that also consisted of Christian Democrats and Socialists. The PRI opposed the bill because it had been excluded from the policy-making process and believed the legislation was poorly designed (Perlmutter 1996).

Union leaders saw the Martelli Law as a step forward in two ways. First, it made the policy-making process much more democratic, injecting interest groups and parliamentary debate into a process that was previously dominated by administrative decree. Second, the law addressed immigration questions more comprehensively than any previous law or decree. For example, it included a broad-based amnesty for illegal immigrants and employers who hired clandestine workers. This legalization process was much better coordinated and publicized than the 1986 amnesty. Restrictions on renewing work and residency permits were relaxed, and an annual quota system was established—with the input of labor unions and employers—to control legal immigration flows.

Union Protest and the Dini Government. The Dini Decree provides the best example of unions successfully using protest to veto restrictive immigration policies. The Dini government was a centrist regime that faced increasing pressure from the right-wing Northern League party and other EU member states to restrict immigration. So, unlike in 1991, unions faced an unfriendly government. Nevertheless, union-led protest not only forced the government to back down on restrictions, but ultimately led policy-makers to change direction and implement an amnesty.

The original intent of the Dini Decree was to increase police powers to detain and expel illegal immigrants, as well as legal immigrants who had committed crimes and were deemed socially dangerous. Under previous legislation police could not detain illegal immigrants. Instead, they could only give the illegal immigrant a summons to report to the local police within fifteen days, after which the immigrant could face deportation. The Dini Decree was issued in November 1995, pending parliamentary approval.

The unions led a protest against the decree in February 1996, a protest that mobilized about 150,000 people against the threat of increased police powers. Many labor leaders conclude that the demonstration convinced the left-wing minority in parliament to vote against the decree, thereby eliminating the most restrictive aspects of the law. In the revised decree, passed by parliament in December 1996, an amnesty and a quota for non-EU seasonal workers were added. As a result, nearly 150,000 illegal immigrants were legalized.

In the Martelli case, labor unions used protest proactively to gain access to the policy-making process and demonstrate the need for immigration reform. Protest helped place immigration reform on the government agenda, and made unions one of the main actors in the policy-making process. In contrast, in the Dini case, labor unions reacted to restrictive policies, which had been made without their input.

Italian Labor Leaders and the 1998 Immigration Reform. In the third and final Italian case, labor leaders refrained from protesting against restrictive aspects of the 1998 immigration bill for fear of upsetting the socialists' majority and thus losing access to the policy-making process.

Although immigration was not a campaign issue in the 1996 elections, immigration reform became a top priority of the new socialist government of Romano Prodi because of Italy's pending entry into the Schengen group, scheduled for April 1998.

By the late 1990s the Martelli Law, although appropriate for its time, had become outdated. As a result, labor leaders wanted a comprehensive immigration reform that addressed both immigration flows and social, economic, and political rights for immigrants in Italy. However, not all of their proposals were adopted. The 1998 law was a compromise between the left—which focused on improving immigrants' social, economic, and political rights—and the right, which wanted to crack down on illegal immigration. Nonetheless, labor was an important actor throughout the policy-making process, and several of its proposals were incorporated into the new law.

Between January and November 1997, the Ministry of Social Solidarity, which cowrote the law, met with the unions three times to discuss their proposals. According to a representative of the ministry, the government relies on unions to provide many social and legal services to immigrants. Therefore, it made sense for the unions to be important partners in the policy-making process.

In addition to formal institutional contacts, the unions also adeptly used informal access to influence the policy-making process. Before the bill was presented to parliament, the unions pressured the government to make quotas available to third-world immigrants by including a fourth, open category in the quota policy. The unions also convinced the government to include the principle of public sponsorship in the new quota system. Initially, the system proposed recognized only private sponsors of immigrants, such as individuals and firms, who could show that the immigrants had some means of financial support. The unions urged that public bodies also have the ability to sponsor immigrants, thus giving the unions a greater role in setting quotas.

Once the legislation was given to parliament, unions shifted their attention to lobbying elected officials for further amendments. For example, the government had proposed a six-year temporary residency period before immigrants could gain permanent residency. Labor leaders wanted to shorten this period and base permanent residency only on length of stay, ignoring income and housing requirements. Ultimately, parliament kept the income and housing requirements but shortened the time requirement to five years.

The unions were pleased with several aspects of the reform, such as the new quota system that finally provided a regular, legal avenue for immigration to Italy, and the creation of permanent residency status. Also, labor leaders approved of reforms that secured social and economic rights for immigrants, such as access to national health services, public schools, and housing.

On the other hand, the unions opposed new powers granted to the local police to decide on renewals of work and residency permits and to grant permanent residency status. Labor leaders also opposed the new detention centers and additional police powers to arrest and detain illegal immigrants. Finally, they were disappointed that the law did not include an amnesty. Instead, the law created a gray area for clandestine immigrants who had arrived before 1998, who could not be immediately legalized or deported. Labor leaders believe the new law represents a compromise by the socialists, a compromise that was needed to get the conservative members of parliament to agree to greater social, economic, and political rights for immigrants.

Some labor leaders wanted unions to protest more vigorously over restrictive aspects of the law. However, others did not want to risk compromising the majority position of the socialists, who had given unions access to the policy-making process. According to one labor leader, the unions were judicious in their criticism because they feared alienating the center-left government, which would have jeopardized the positive aspects of the law (author interview, Adriana Buffardi, President, IRES/CGIL, Rome, December 16, 1997).

Conclusion

Because the immigration policy-making process is complex, involving many domestic and international actors, it is difficult to show a direct causal relationship between labor union actions and policy change. Nevertheless, a pattern of increasing openness in immigration is evident when the immigration preferences of labor leaders are translated into action.

The clearest examples of the relationship between labor union action and policy change are the two Italian cases from 1990 and 1995. In the Martelli case, the effects of labor-led protest were rewarded almost immediately with access to the policy-making process and reforms that met the demands of labor. Similarly, the initial Dini Decree was met with large labor-led protests, followed by parliamentary rejection of the decree and a rewrite that included an amnesty.

The effects of labor union influence in the 1996 Spanish immigration reform are less clear because the reform process was more protracted. Nonetheless, Spanish labor unions were the main societal actors who brought discrepancies in the 1985 LOE to the attention of policy-makers through protest, proposals, and petitions. Because of pressure exerted by unions and union expertise in migration issues, the socialist government included them in the 1995–1996 reform process, which resulted in the implementation of many union proposals.

Changes in French immigration policy could be explained simply by changes in government. However, the French immigration policy-making process is considerably more complex. As in Spain and Italy today, the CGT and the CFDT provided the main channel for immigrants to voice their concerns to policy-makers in the 1970s. The CGT, for example, was instrumental in winning workplace rights for immigrants in 1972 and 1974. But in the late 1970s union protests failed to block restrictive measures imposed by conservative governments. The election of a socialist government committed to the cause of labor unions and immigrant associations was the necessary condition for policy moderation in France. Likewise, labor leaders claim little influence on the 1998 immigration reform, which was inspired by the election of a socialist majority. The purpose of the 1998 law was to find common ground between the right and the left on immigration reform, thus giving France a workable immigration policy. However, in finding a compromise position the socialist government alienated the left, including the CGT and CFDT. Nevertheless, union efforts have helped mold the immigration debate. For example, labor leaders have checked the influence of the anti-immigrant National Front through campaigns to educate and train labor militants and workers about racism and discrimination against immigrants. Although the influence of French labor unions may not be as apparent as in the Italian and Spanish cases, they have had an important long-term effect on the policy-making process.

Despite formidable constraints on labor's ability to moderate immigration policy—namely, poor economic performance and the "securitization" of immigration policy—labor leaders influence the domestic immigration policy-making process. However, in the near future, immigration policy will no longer be the exclusive domain of European states.

As a result of the 1997 Amsterdam Treaty, competency for immigration policy is being transferred from nation states and intergovernmental bodies to the institutions of the European Union. Prior to Amsterdam, intergovernmental discussions of immigration policy were shrouded in secrecy and focused on security and policing concerns. Granting authority for immigration policy to the European Commission promises to make the policy-making process more open and transparent. This important shift, which is the subject of the next chapter, poses challenges and opportunities for labor union leaders, who must now broaden their scope to the European level.

6

Forging a Common European Immigration Policy

hanges in the global economy have caused aspects of national immigration policies to converge. Technological advances have made global communication and transportation more accessible to legal and illegal immigrant networks. This, in turn, challenges the states' ability to control immigration effectively. Fearing a crisis of immigration control, government officials in Europe and elsewhere in the industrialized world are developing and enforcing more stringent border control policies to stem illegal immigration.[1]

At the same time, economic competition from developing countries has sharpened employer demand for flexible, low-cost immigrant labor willing to do precarious work that natives shun in the textile, agriculture, construction, and service sectors. Countries that face acute labor shortages are experimenting with immigration policies that help meet that problem such as employment-based quotas and bilateral agreements with sending states.

---

[1] According to Cornelius, Martin, and Hollifield (1994) government officials were less confident in the early 1990s about their ability to effectively regulate immigration than they had been fifteen years earlier. Also, according to a recent OECD report, in several OECD countries measures have been implemented to combat irregular immigration and the illegal employment of immigrants (OECD 1999).

Despite these challenges, formal multilateral coordination on immigration is rare because states do not want to cede control over an issue so central to the notion of national sovereignty. The only exception is the European Union (EU), where member states are gradually moving toward a common European immigration policy. According to the president of the European Commission, Romano Prodi, "The European Council's plans to harmonize member state immigration policies mark a new step in the European Union after the common market, common currency and Schengen" (European Council Summit, Tampere, Finland, October 16, 1999). However, EU member states have conflicting interests between protecting their sovereign control over immigration policy and completing the single European market by removing all barriers to the free movement of goods, services, capital and people within the community.

In this chapter, I return to the question of immigration policy convergence, but from a different perspective, that of convergence among the EU member states. The harmonization of internal market policies among these states is often interpreted as a continuous progression toward eliminating trade barriers in goods, services, money, and labor. But despite the potential economic gains of a free labor market, many member states have been reluctant to pool control over immigration in Community institutions, because member states view immigration from outside the EU, or third-country immigration, in the context of national security concerns.

Also, EU member states have diverse economic and political interests and unique experiences with regard to immigration. Southern European countries have relatively short histories of immigration compared to many of their northern neighbors. As a result, southern European countries are still developing immigration policies to fit their economic needs. At the same time, policy-makers in some Northern European countries are struggling to cope with the incorporation of permanent immigrant populations and questions of national identity.

Despite different national interests, EU member states have agreed to move control of immigration policy from the domain of individual states and intergovernmental institutions to Community institutions. However, they qualified this transfer of authority from the intergovernmental "Third Pillar" to the Community "First Pillar" by requiring that decisions be made unanimously and providing for member states to opt out of directives during a five-year transition period. According to the Treaty of Amsterdam, ratified in 1999, the European Commission and individual member states share the right to initiate proposals concerning immigration to the Council of the European Union, which acts on proposals by unanimous vote. In 2004, the Commission will gain the sole right of initiative, but it must consider proposals made by member states. The European Parliament gains only a consultory role in the process. Thus, at least temporarily, the member states have protected their national prerogative to make immigration policy by incorporating flexibility and unanimity, aspects of the Third Pillar, into the First Pillar.

As a result, the future of immigration policy-making in the EU is open to interpretation. Romano Prodi, Commission president, argues that "national administrations should put aside any residual nostalgia for the days of pure intergovernmentalism which Amsterdam finally laid to rest"(European Council 1999). At the same time, the British remain intransigent about abolishing internal frontier controls and claim that enhanced visa cooperation would create difficulties for the United Kingdom.[2]

Three questions are explored in this chapter. First, how have intergovernmental agreements among the EU member states evolved into Community policies? Second, what is the relationship between policy-making at the domestic and European levels? Third, what role will national employers' associations and labor unions play in influencing policy at the European level?

Sovereign Control over Immigration Policy vs. Community Institutions

Three theoretical frameworks shed light on why immigration policy is being transferred from intergovernmental to Community institutions. The first follows the functional logic expressed by President Prodi, that free movement of people is the next step in European unification.

[2] Announcement by the British Home Secretary at a European Council Justice and Home Affairs Meeting, March 1999 (Cruz 1999).

Functionalists argue that since internal borders for goods, services, and people have been eliminated among the member states, it is also necessary to have a consistent policy with regard to immigration from outside the EU. Ernst Haas (1958) first used the functional approach to explain the path of European unification in the 1950s. According to Haas, policy-makers who realize the benefits of cooperating in one area will apply these lessons to new situations, creating a "spill-over" effect that ultimately leads to harmonized policies at the European level.

Member states want to realize the economic benefits of eliminating internal borders, which requires that they cooperate on external border controls. By sharing information and pooling resources in the areas of policing, police training, and prosecution, member states can better regulate their external borders. In practice, the process of finding common ground on immigration has not been as fluid as the functional approach predicts. Decision-making "spill-over" from one issue area to another, in this case from the internal market to immigration policy, is a necessary but not sufficient explanation for the transference of authority for immigration policy to Community institutions.

The second framework focuses on institutional credibility and capacity. The primary European institution for immigration, the Schengen Group, lacked credibility in the eyes of European citizens because its decisions were made in secret with no input from interest groups or elected officials. Yet immigration is a major concern of Europeans—witness the 1999 electoral success of the extreme right in Austria. Hence, tackling the immigration issue became central to the legitimacy of the EU and required the incorporation of Schengen into the more transparent Community framework. For example, at a special meeting of the European Council on immigration issues, President Prodi said the Council must send a message to its citizens that "we are genuinely determined to devote our energies to matters which directly affect [EU citizens] in their daily lives"(European Council 1999).

Also, because Schengen began as an intergovernmental agreement among a subset of EU member states, it lacked the institutional capacity to function effectively in an expanded Europe of up to twenty-seven members with increasingly porous eastern and southern borders. Not only would eastern enlargement seriously challenge the policing, informational, and training capacities of Schengen, it also would require additional translators and meeting space. Given these challenges, the Schengen Group needed financial and technical support from the EU to survive.

These functional and institutional explanations provide the backdrop to understanding why competency for immigration policy should be transferred to Community institutions. However, since the mid-1980s, efforts to coordinate immigration policies have been characterized by complex intergovernmental negotiations among EU member states. According to Keohane and Hoffman (1991), negotiating and coalition-building within the EU takes place between governments, not in the context of supranational institutions. In other words, policy convergence begins with domestic political processes and interstate bargaining, and is most successful when the preferences of governments are similar. Whether policies in fact converge is determined by negotiations among member states and domestic cost-benefit analyses.

In the case of immigration, member states have realized that eliminating internal borders is essential to achieving the full economic benefits of a common market. But this also requires closer cooperation on external border control to keep out illegal immigrants, drug traffickers, and money launderers. Nevertheless, for many years, the "spill-over" effect could not surmount differences among EU member states. Rather, a protracted process of intergovernmental bargaining that began in the mid-1980s made immigration a Community competency. At the 1997 Amsterdam Intergovernmental Conference, the member states negotiated an agreement that addresses institutional weaknesses while protecting their license to make immigration policy.

From Schengen to Amsterdam: A Case Study in Intergovernmental Bargaining

Although the free movement of people among the EU member states was a founding principle of the 1957 Treaty of Rome, progress toward harmonizing immigration policies has been incremental. In fact, immigration was not identified as a key social policy of the Community until 1974, when the European Council adopted an action plan for migrant workers and their families. And, until the mid-1980s, immigration policy largely ignored non-EU immigrants, with the exception of bilateral nondiscrimination agreements between the European Community and immigrant sending states, such as Turkey, Algeria, Morocco, Tunisia, and the former Yugoslavia. These treaties guaranteed equal treatment for immigrants and natives with regard to social security, employment, and pay.

By the mid-1980s, several member states began to appreciate their common economic and security interests concerning third-country immigration. However, within the domain of EU institutions, the necessary unanimous consensus was missing because of opposition from the United Kingdom, Denmark, and Ireland. These countries argued that free movement should apply only to nationals of EU member states. They opposed eliminating internal border checks, a step which would give third-country immigrants de facto free mobility once inside the EU.

As a result, a subset of member states created an extra-EU intergovernmental body, the Schengen Group. The impetus came from German commercial truck drivers, who wanted to expedite interstate trade but were deluged by border check inspections. In 1984, the German government took the initiative and unilaterally relaxed its border controls. Shortly thereafter, Germany signed a bilateral border agreement with France. In 1985, this bilateral arrangement was transformed into the Schengen Agreements. France, Germany, Belgium, Luxembourg, and the Netherlands became the original members. Later, the Schengen Club expanded to include Italy, Spain, Portugal, Greece, Austria, Sweden, and Finland.

The Schengen Agreements are not common immigration policies, but rather common border policies. Nevertheless, Schengen evolved into more than an agreement on border controls and became a "laboratory" for European immigration policy. The Agreements sought to abolish internal border controls gradually, while reinforcing external borders. For example, inspections at internal border crossings were eliminated, and customs police may apprehend suspects in another member state's jurisdiction. At the same time, the Schengen Agreements strengthen external controls by clarifying and tightening asylum rules so that refugees cannot apply for asylum in more than one member state. In addition, Schengen members created a common visa list and coordinated police surveillance at external border checks.

Various obstacles complicated negotiations over how to implement Schengen. These challenges included the reunification of East and West Germany, reconciliation of different national policies on the possession of soft drugs, data protection, and bank secrecy (Baldwin-Edwards and Schain 1994, 179). Because of differences among the Schengen member states, the Agreements were only partially implemented in June 1990, and further implementation was repeatedly delayed. For example, Italy did not gain full membership until April 1998 because until that time, other Schengen members, concerned about Italy's porous borders and its unwillingness to deport illegal immigrants, blocked its entry. Italy was admitted shortly after its new immigration law addressed these concerns in March 1998. As part of the 1997 Amsterdam Treaty, the member states agreed to incorporate Schengen into the First Pillar of the EU. This means that immigration control will be transferred gradually from intergovernmental institutions, which are characterized by unanimity, secrecy, and opaqueness, to more open and democratic Community institutions. From a functional perspective, one could argue that the Schengen member states realized the economic benefits of cooperating on border control and therefore agreed to further pool their sovereignty in Community institutions, where majority rule facilitates the decision-making process. However, some EU officials cite institutional overload as a reason for transferring Schengen to Community institutions. Institutionally, the Schengen Group had grown too cumbersome to function autonomously. For example, adding new members required additional translators and larger meeting space. According to a Commission official, Schengen needed the financial and technical support that EU institutions could provide. More important, the challenge of controlling Schengen's porous southern border seems insignificant in the face of the imminent expansion of the EU into Central Europe.

The Schengen Agreements also lacked credibility because they failed to establish a democratic or transparent decision-making process. Because immigration is a highly politicized issue among European citizens, it was essential for the EU to send a "clear political message to Europe's citizens" that immigration was a priority.[3]

Member states and EU officials have not yet fully appreciated the consequences of transferring Schengen into the EU institutional framework. For example, sensitive decisions regarding border control that were once made in secret will now be published in the Official Journal of the European Commission. At the October 1999 European Council Summit in Tampere, Finland, member state representatives avoided the issue of mobility for third-country nationals because it was considered "too controversial."[4] Also, some councils and positions within Schengen will be eliminated as intergovernmental bodies are divided and reassigned.

Institutional concerns with Schengen's capacity and credibility helped push the member states to negotiate an agreement at Amsterdam that would move Schengen into the Community framework. However, reaching an agreement that satisfied the demands of all the member states required introducing intergovernmental procedures that may corrupt the First Pillar approach. For example, for the first five years that immigration is a Community competency, decisions must be made unanimously. Britain, Denmark, and Ireland also negotiated an opt-out, or flexibility, clause that allows member states in the minority to ignore majority decisions. Essentially, the flexibility clause requires unanimous voting. In this sense, immigration is not a true First Pillar concern. Instead, member states, for the time being, have retained some control over immigration policy by combining aspects of the Third and First Pillars.

The Schengen case demonstrates that EU member states have a common economic interest in completing the internal market, as well as a common political interest in regulating third-country immigration. However, creating Schengen and incorporating it into the EU framework was not inevitable. Rather, these processes were characterized by intergovernmental bargaining and institutional concerns. Member

[3] Speech by Nicole Fontaine, President of the European Parliament, at a Special Meeting of the European Council, Tampere, Finland, October 1999.

[4] Prime Minister of Finland Paavo Lipponen at the Presidency Press Conference, Tampere, Finland, October 1999.

states have preferred to retain control of their borders and immigration policies. They therefore have incorporated immigration policy into Community institutions in such a way that their sovereignty cannot easily be jeopardized.

Member State Immigration Policies and European Initiatives

Domestic immigration policy has served as a laboratory, as well as a catalyst, for European initiatives. For example, when the German government unilaterally relaxed its border with France in 1984 to expedite cross-border trade, its neighbors quickly followed suit, and the resulting Schengen Agreements became a testing ground for European-wide immigration policies. After many years of intergovernmental negotiations, the German initiative became part of the EU with the ratification of the Amsterdam Treaty in 1999.

In September 1999, the Spanish government signed an agreement with Morocco, which permits up to 300,000 Moroccans per year to work in Spanish agriculture and construction. Guest workers are granted nine-month work permits, and after four years of seasonal work they can obtain more long-term immigrant status. The bilateral agreement is expected to serve as a model for agreements planned between Spain and Colombia, Ecuador, Mali, Romania, and Poland. It also has important implications for other EU member states. Moroccan migrants who enter Spain also enter the EU because Spain is a member of Schengen. At the signing, Morocco's minister of labor, Khalid Alioua, said this is "the first agreement of this type. It is an important agreement. It was signed with a country that is a member of the Schengen area [and] introduces a new approach in managing migration into Europe. [Spain] admits workers into the European space, even on the temporary basis. Therefore, it is responsible toward other European nations." Morocco hopes to conclude similar agreements with Italy, Belgium, the Netherlands, and France (Migration News Sheet 1999).

At the October 1999 European Council Summit in Tampere, Finland, member states agreed in principle to partnerships with third countries that promote co-development. However, member state representatives left undecided the issue of free movement of legal immigrants in the

EU, which was seen as too controversial an issue. Bilateral agreements between EU member states that want migrant labor and immigrant sending states will quicken the speed at which the EU develops partnerships with third countries. In addition, these agreements will force member states to decide whether to sanction, on an official basis, the free movement of legal immigrants within the EU.

Domestic immigration policies, bilateral agreements between immigrant sending states and EU member states, and agreements among member states have shaped efforts to build a common European immigration policy. However, immigration policies are not always initiated at the domestic level to later shape EU policies.

European Pressures on Domestic Immigration Policy

Pressures to conform and join the club have compelled some member states to alter their immigration policies. Typically, these changes have meant imposing stricter controls on illegal immigration in southern Europe under the watchful eye of northern Europe. This is particularly true in Italy and Spain, new countries of immigration with relatively weak control mechanisms. Eager to join the Schengen club, Spain and Italy had to tighten their border controls to assure their neighbors that illegal immigrants would not pass through on their way north.

Grete Brochmann (1996, 98) argues that the mere existence of the European Community influences the policies of its individual member states: "The Community has a significant indirect impact because governments must consider other states' policies due to the international character of current migration flows." According to Brochmann, immigration policies will converge toward the policy of the most restrictive state to avoid the "magnet effect" of attracting non-EU immigrants.

Two examples from Italy and Spain demonstrate that the EU exerts an important influence on domestic immigration policy-making. However, immigration policies are not necessarily becoming more restrictive, as Brochmann predicts. Instead, Italy and Spain are balancing their economic needs for immigrant labor and political concerns for integrating immigrants with external demands to control illegal immigration.

Spain and the 1985 Ley de Extranjeria

Two external forces stimulated Spanish government officials to pass a restrictive immigration policy in 1985: the government needed to respond to the increasing numbers of immigrants arriving in Spain, and it needed to adapt its legislation to fit Community guidelines (Aragón Bombin 1996). The government passed the Ley de Extranjeria (LOE) on July 1, 1985, just days after Spain signed the treaty for accession to the European Community. The 1985 law resulted from negotiations related to Spain's entry and pressure from other member states to restrict immigration from outside the Community (Calavita 1997; Casey 1998).

Generally speaking, measures in the LOE that regulated the entry of third-country immigrants into Spain were strict enough to meet the requirements of the Schengen Agreements, which Spain signed in June 1990. However, the negative effects of the restrictive 1985 LOE demonstrated to policy-makers, employers, and labor leaders that a zero immigration policy was unrealistic for Spain given the demands of its labor market and its proximity to North Africa. The reforms of 1991, 1996, and 1999 illustrate how policy-makers have tried to stay within the bounds of intergovernmental agreements by pursuing a controlled immigration policy that seeks to reduce illegal immigration, but at the same time, meet Spain's labor market needs by legalizing illegal immigrants and channeling immigrant workers to sectors that face labor shortages (author interview, Roman Garcia, Sub-Director for Immigration, Ministry of Labor and Social Affairs, Madrid, November 16, 1996).

Schengen and the Italian Crack-Down on Illegal Immigration

The continuing problem of illegal immigration, combined with a desire to gain full membership in Schengen, stimulated the Italian government to draft new immigration legislation in 1998. Previous legislation provided few opportunities for legal immigration to Italy, yet control mechanisms were notoriously weak. As a result, Italy repeatedly has used amnesties to reduce the size of its illegal immigrant population, and these measures may have further stimulated illegal immigration.

Italy's 1998 law seeks to be comprehensive by balancing external control policies with an internal expansion of social, economic, and political rights for legal immigrants. At the same time, the law is a compromise between the left, which favors more open immigration policies, and the right, which wants to restrict immigration and strengthen controls.

Italy's policy of issuing deportation orders, but not detaining illegal immigrants, was a stumbling block to full membership in Schengen. Not surprisingly, most illegal immigrants failed to turn themselves into the Italian authorities, and many proceeded to northern Europe. Therefore, the Italian government was under pressure to crack down on illegal entries to gain full membership in Schengen by the April 1998 deadline.

The new law, passed in March 1998, strengthened police powers to arrest illegal immigrants and created immigrant detention centers. Under Article 12, immigrants who enter Italy without proper documentation, but cannot be expelled immediately, are to be placed in detention centers until their expulsion date. Detained immigrants are given the right of defense and cannot be held for more than twenty days without legal action.

According to Francesco Lanata of the Italian Ministry of Foreign Affairs, Italy's pending membership in Schengen gave greater urgency to strengthening border controls. But Italy, like Spain, faces labor shortages in specific sectors as well as a large illegal immigrant population. Consequently, policy-makers sought to balance pressures to restrict illegal immigration with the demands of the Italian economy for immigrant labor by creating a more expansive quota policy.

When it came to legalizing illegal immigrants, the Italian government was reluctant to hold another amnesty before Italy gained full membership in Schengen. Consequently, policy-makers intentionally avoided the amnesty issue in the 1998 law. However, according to the law, immigrants who entered Italy illegally prior to March 1998 cannot be expelled. Since March 1998, the undefined legal status of many immigrants has been remedied by two amnesties. In the fall of 1998, 38,000 work permits were granted to employed immigrants who arrived before March. Approximately 280,000 undocumented immigrants applied. The Ministry of the Interior promised those who met the requirements, but were not granted a permit in 1998, that they could stay in Italy and become eligible for the 1999 quota. In February 1999, Italy offered a second amnesty in which 300,000 immigrants applied and 150,000 received legal status (Migration News Sheet 1999).

Because full membership in Schengen was important to Italians, who no longer wanted to be thought of as second-tier members of the club, European pressures were a significant impetus for the 1998 law. Still, policy-makers sought to balance the needs of the Italian economy and the integration of immigrants against external demands to restrict illegal immigration.

These two cases demonstrate that Europe exerts an important influence over the domestic immigration policy-making process. For Spain and Italy, membership in the "club" often has required the adoption of more stringent border control policies to demonstrate to other member states that controlling illegal immigration is a priority. However, Spain and Italy have their own specific economic and political immigration concerns. Contrary to Brochmann's prediction, member states are not converging toward the policy of the most restrictive state. Immigration policies in Spain and Italy demonstrate that states seek to stay within the bounds of European agreements and satisfy the demands of unions and employers for more moderate policies.

The question of who will control the immigration policy-making process remains unanswered, since authority for immigration policy is shifting from intergovernmental to Community institutions. To date, domestic policies and agreements among states have propelled efforts to forge a common European immigration policy. At the same time, domestic policy-makers, who wish to realize the economic and security benefits of participating in European agreements, must consider pressures emanating from EU and intergovernmental institutions. Still, member states have been reluctant to yield control over immigration policy to Community institutions. Despite the message of the Amsterdam Treaty, that immigration will be a true First Pillar concern by 2004, immigration policy-making will continue to be a contentious issue among member states, and between member states and Community institutions.

Investigating the connections between domestic and European immigration policy-making has important theoretical implications. This research would afford the opportunity to develop and test theories that explain simultaneous interactions between domestic and international actors. Analyses that link supranational and domestic negotiations could help discern how supranational negotiations affect domestic policy choices, how member states form coalitions and link issues, and how interest groups such as business and labor influence supranational negotiations.

Labor Union and Employer Influence at the EU Level

As a result of the Amsterdam Treaty, the European immigration policy-making process will become more complex for labor unions and employers, but also more transparent and accessible.

National labor unions and employers' associations are represented in Brussels through supranational bodies, the European Trade Union Confederation (ETUC) and the Union of Industry Confederations and Employers of Europe (UNICE). And the Commission regularly consults with these organizations and their members under the auspices of the "Social Partners."

Prior to the Amsterdam Treaty, the Commission had no competency for making immigration policy. As a result, unions and employer organizations struggled to discuss immigration concretely on the European level. The ETUC has a section dedicated to migration issues, but policy debates have focused mainly on fighting racism and discrimination in the workplace. And UNICE did not take a position on third-country immigration with the exception of social security benefits for third-country immigrants. Nevertheless, in 1992 the Commission, unions, and employers indirectly addressed immigration by examining problems of racism and discrimination in the workplace under the auspices of the Social Charter. In 1995, employers and unions signed the Joint Declaration for the Prevention of Racial Discrimination and Xenophobia and Promotion of Equal Treatment in the Workplace. This declaration led to a study called the "Compendium of Good Practice for the Prevention of Racism in the Workplace," meant to influence future EU policies dealing with racism and discrimination.

The Amsterdam Treaty opens the possibility for employers and unions to address immigration questions directly through the Commission. However, both ETUC and UNICE believe the transfer of authority for immigration will proceed slowly and under the direction of the member states (author interviews, Carolyn Croft, Department of Social Affairs, UNICE, Brussels, December 12, 1997, and Maria Helena André, Confederal Secretary, ETUC, Brussels, September 23, 1997). The ETUC foresees greater opportunities to influence immigration policy at the EU level than does UNICE, which, although it strongly supports measures to facilitate the free movement of workers, has not taken a position on third-country immigration.

UNICE has not done so for two reasons. First, its employers believe lobbying efforts are wasted at the European level as long as immigration remains in the hands of member states. Second, UNICE members believe third-country immigration does not directly affect company concerns, with the exception of their need to provide social security benefits for immigrants and fight racism in the workplace (interview, Carolyn Croft). In these areas, UNICE has written briefing papers and signed on to European-wide agreements, such as the Joint Declaration on the Prevention of Racial Discrimination in the Workplace. And, with regard to pensions, UNICE supports initiatives to ensure that workers moving from one member state to another are not treated differently from workers moving within a single member state.

One of the biggest challenges facing labor unions and employers' associations is how to move beyond national priorities and processes to the European level. Unions have found common ground on some issues, such as eradicating discrimination against immigrants in the workplace. However, the national labor unions are divided on the problem of illegal immigration and its connection to the underground economy. Southern European unions support amnesties as a way to reduce both the number of illegal immigrants and the size of the underground economy. On the other hand, northern European unions do not believe legalization is an appropriate solution to underground employment. They often ignore the problem of underground work because their underground economies are more modest and because illegal immigrants make up a smaller portion of total employment.

For labor unions and employers' associations, the main avenue to influence immigration policy is through the Commission. However, their level of influence largely depends on how much initiative the Commission assumes in the policy-making process. According to a communication from the Commission's Directorate General for Justice and Home Affairs, "the Commission is prepared to act as a catalyst and make a practical contribution to the member states' efforts to construct a common asylum and immigration regime"(European Commission 2000). To this end, the Commission has made several proposals on third-country immigration, including temporary protection status for refugees, family reunification, visa regulation, and revision of the Dublin Convention on asylum and illegal immigration. In addition, the Commission has set up a "scoreboard" or timetable for immigration reform that is meant to confront member states with their responsibilities and ensure democratic scrutiny and transparency.

Through protracted negotiations among the member states over more than ten years, a common European immigration policy is visible on the horizon. As authority for immigration is transferred from inter-governmental institutions to EU institutions, the immigration policy-making process should become more transparent and open to input from interest groups. But until 2004, the member states will continue to shape immigration policy at the European level through the Council, unanimous voting requirements, and the flexibility clause. Ultimately, these conditions may weaken the First Pillar approach.

7

Reflections on the U.S. Case

On April 12 and May 15, 2000, U.S. business and labor leaders met in Washington, D.C., to discuss strategies for easing the nation's immigration laws. The goal of the meetings was to build a broad-based coalition to lobby for reforms, such as increased admitting of skilled immigrants, an amnesty for undocumented immigrants, and additional visas for family reunification. Attendees included the Essential Workers Immigration Coalition (EWIC), an alliance of businesses concerned with the shortage of skilled and unskilled workers; the Service Employees International Union (SEIU); the Hotel Employees and Restaurant Employees International Union (HERE); United Farm Workers of America (UFW); and the Union of Needletrades and Industrial Textile Employees (UNITE).

This loose coalition of business and labor was made possible when the AFL-CIO reversed its stance on employer sanctions and amnesties in February 2000. Previously, the AFL-CIO advocated government sanctions against employers who knowingly hired illegal immigrants, and was silent on legalizing the undocumented. Although some regional and sectoral union leaders had been discussing immigration reform since the mid-1990s, this movement did not reach the national level until the October 1999 AFL-CIO National Convention in Los Angeles. At the convention, some of the most aggressive and fastest-growing unions, such as SEIU, UNITE, UFW, and HERE, called for an end to the current system of employer sanctions and a blanket amnesty for undocumented immigrants.

Although the AFL-CIO was not yet ready to pass a new immigration resolution at the convention, leaders recognized that the current system of employer sanctions was a failure, and wanted to respond to demands from immigrant workers for a new amnesty. As a result, the union leadership appointed a special immigration commission headed by John Wilhelm, president of HERE, to study the issues further. Soon after, in February 2000, the Executive Committee of the AFL-CIO resolved to abolish the system of employer sanctions created by the 1986 Immigration Reform and Control Act (IRCA), and to secure a blanket amnesty for undocumented immigrants.

Meanwhile, historically low unemployment rates put both high-tech and low-tech employers on the lobbying offensive to increase skilled and unskilled immigration and to legalize undocumented immigrant workers. In fact, Alan Greenspan, chairman of the U.S. Federal Reserve Board, has advised policy-makers to admit more immigrant workers to avoid labor shortages that could lead to wage pressures and inflation. This combination of factors has opened a unique window of opportunity for labor and business to form a powerful lobbying coalition to increase legal immigration and legalize hundreds of thousands of undocumented immigrants.

Time will tell whether this coalition becomes a political force. Because the AFL-CIO's immigration reversal is so recent and dramatic, labor and business are still reflecting on what the change will mean in terms of policy. For example, labor leaders have called for an end to the current system of employer sanctions, but have not formulated an alternative system. Opposed to employer sanctions and seeking more immigrant workers, many employers are hopeful about the AFL-CIO's new stance. At the same time, they are wary of what labor might propose to replace employer sanctions (author interview, John Gay, Co-Chair, EWIC, October 2000). As a result, only tentative conclusions can be drawn about how this coalition may affect the immigration policy-making process.

Nevertheless, the changing immigration policy preferences of the AFL-CIO's leadership can be explained using variables similar to those that account for labor's positions in Spain, Italy, and France. In the United States, as in Europe, the liberalization of preferences can be explained by:

- labor leaders' lack of confidence in the state's capacity to control immigration,
- union organization and membership, and
- economic marginalization of immigrant workers in the secondary economy.

Largely absent from the AFL-CIO's revised position is an ideological rationale based on the belief that all workers—natives, immigrants, and potential migrants—are part of an international class struggle. Instead, the AFL-CIO's support for more open immigration policies is based on a much more practical foundation—the realization that U.S. immigration policy is "broken and needs to be fixed" (AFL-CIO 2000c). Rather than discouraging employers from hiring undocumented immigrants or stopping the flow of illegal immigrants, restrictive immigration policies have marginalized immigrant workers by placing them in precarious legal and employment situations. This in turn prevents many immigrant workers from joining unions for fear of employer retaliation, while at the same time it undercuts the wages and working conditions of natives. Even more than those of their French, Spanish, and Italian counterparts, U.S. labor leaders' immigration preferences are based on a pragmatic analysis of how the current system of immigration laws harms immigrant and native workers, and of how to arrest declining union membership rates.

On the business side, U.S. employers, who are openly pro-immigration, offer an interesting contrast to their more ambivalent European counterparts. For the last several years, low unemployment and rapid economic growth have contributed to their pro-immigration position. But even in periods of slow growth, American employers have lobbied to increase, or at least maintain, immigration numbers. This is in part because U.S. immigration policy is discussed in terms that directly affect employers—numbers and sanctions—rather than in terms of immigrant integration policies. Also, without European-style national employers' associations, U.S. employers can act as free agents in government lobbying. When interests converge around industry-specific legislation, employers are free to form powerful lobbying groups such as the Information Technology Association of America (ITAA) and the National Council of Agricultural Employers. For example, despite inconclusive evidence of a long-term shortage of information technology (IT) workers, in 1998 and 2000 ITAA lobbying efforts helped IT companies secure thousands of additional visas for highly skilled immigrant workers.

A brief discussion of U.S. immigration policy since the 1960s sheds some light on how labor leaders' and employers' policy preferences have evolved. Today labor leaders are reacting to a series of poorly devised policies that have encouraged illegal immigration and placed immigrant workers in a precarious employment situation. Employers, on the other hand, have participated actively in the immigration policy-making process for many years. Consequently, they have become politically adept at increasing, or at least maintaining, legal immigration numbers.

U.S. Immigration Policy since the Mid-1960s

Gaps between policies intended to control immigration and immigration outcomes are not peculiar to the United States. As discussed in Chapter 3, these gaps are common to most immigrant-receiving countries. Unintended outcomes of immigration policies often result from external pressures, such as increasing economic openness in developing countries. In the short run, economic instability may stimulate even more emigration, as was the case with the Mexican financial crisis in the 1990s. Also, domestic pressures to restrict immigration may conflict with fundamental human rights guaranteed by liberal democracies.

In addition, several major pieces of poorly devised and poorly enforced immigration legislation inadvertently have promoted illegal immigration to the United States. Between 1942 and 1964, about 4.6 million Mexicans came north across the border as temporary farm labor under the Bracero Program. Many policy-makers believed that a legal guest worker program would reduce illegal immigration. However, 4.9 million undocumented Mexicans were apprehended during the Bracero years. At one point, the Mexican government asked the United States to impose employer sanctions to discourage illegal emigration, but the "Texas Proviso" in the 1952 Immigration and Nationality Act specifically absolved from punishment employers who knowingly hired unauthorized workers. In response to growing opposition from labor unions and civil rights groups, the Bracero Program was allowed to expire in 1964. But following its termination, seasonal migration from Mexico became almost entirely a flow of undocumented immigrants (Lee 1998).

The 1965 Immigration and Nationality Act (INA) also contributed to a rise in illegal immigration in the 1970s. Although the INA purported to eliminate preferential treatment for European emigrants and place new emphasis on the humanitarian goal of family reunification, the law had unintended consequences. By abolishing the national origins visa system in favor of uniform quotas, the United States, for the first time, effectively capped immigration from the Western Hemisphere.[1] As a result, illegal immigration became the only option for many seasonal migrants from Mexico.

By the end of the 1970s, illegal immigration had become a significant concern to policy-makers. In 1978, Congress established the Select Commission on Immigration and Refugee Policy (SCRIP). The Commission called for the immediate closing of the "half-open door of undocumented immigration"(Lee 1998, 69), and proposed to achieve this through better enforcement of border controls, sanctions against employers who hire illegal immigrants, and legalizing some illegal immigrants already in the United States. By closing the back door to illegal immigration, the Commission hoped to open "the front door a little more to accommodate legal immigration in the interests of the country"(Lee 1998, 69). These recommendations served as the blueprint for the 1986 Immigration Reform and Control Act (IRCA) and the 1990 Immigration Act.

---

[1] In 1965, a general Western Hemisphere visa cap was set at 120,000 per year. In 1976, a 20,000 per-year, per-country quota was set for Western Hemisphere countries.

The 1986 act dealt almost exclusively with illegal immigration. It established tighter border controls, an employer sanctions system, and two legalization programs. The first legalization program was a general amnesty that granted permanent residency to undocumented immigrants who had resided in the United States since January 1, 1982. The second amnesty program, Special Agricultural Worker (SAW), allowed certain undocumented immigrants working in agriculture to legalize their status. A total of 3 million immigrants applied for amnesty, with approval rates in the general amnesty of 98 percent and in the SAW program of 94 percent.

In addition, IRCA sought to reduce the demand for illegal immigrants by establishing a system of sanctions that penalized employers who knowingly hired immigrants not authorized to work in the United States. However, the employer sanctions system was flawed from the outset because it was a symbolic measure passed by a Congress that was pressed to do something about illegal immigration but reluctant to aggravate employers (Calavita 1998, 93). As a result, IRCA makes it illegal to knowingly employ aliens not authorized to work in the United States, but it gives employers considerable enforcement authority by making them responsible for verifying workers' documents. Congressional proponents of employer sanctions knew that the INS was capable of monitoring only a fraction of employers, but they believed that most employers would voluntarily comply with the law rather than take the risk of being fined. In 1988, the INS expected to audit approximately 20,000 employers, or one-third of one percent of approximately 7 million employers. However, the INS fell far short of even this modest goal, completing only 12,319 inspections (Calavita 1998, 97–98).

What's more, employers enjoy legal protection from sanctions through the I-9 compliance mechanism. All new employees are required to fill out an I-9 form and provide supporting documentation that proves their right to work in the United States. However, simply completing the I-9 paperwork and checking whether the documentation appears genuine fulfills an employer's responsibility under the law. In other words, Congress made compliance pragmatically easy to persuade employers to support IRCA. And this tactic was in fact successful. In 1985, the U.S. Chamber of Commerce officially endorsed employer sanctions (Calavita 1998, 100).

INS statistics seemed to show that IRCA was working to control illegal immigration. For example, the INS reported that illegal alien apprehensions fell from a high of 1,767,400 in 1986 to 954,243 in 1989. As a result, in the late 1980s policy-makers moved forward to tackle the
second half of the SCRIP Report, which dealt with legal immigration.

Rather than "opening the door a little" to legal immigration, the 1990
Immigration Act increased annual immigration quotas by nearly 40
percent (to 700,000) during fiscal years 1992–1994, and to 675,000 for
fiscal year 1995 and after. Of these 675,000 immigrants, 71 percent
(480,000) were family-sponsored, 21 percent (140,000) were employment-based, and 8 percent (55,000) were "diversity immigrants."[2]

But although policy-makers believed that IRCA and the INS had got-
ten illegal immigration under control, that door actually remained
open. In fact, the reduction in illegal alien apprehensions between 1986
and 1989 may have been less a result of border enforcement and employer sanctions than an effect of the amnesty program. In 1990, illegal
alien apprehensions rose again to 1,169,939. And by the mid-1990s, a
rising share—at least 30 to 40 percent—of farm workers were unauthorized (Martin 1998, 1).

By 1995 the political climate surrounding immigration had changed
dramatically. Emboldened by public support of California's Proposi-
tion 187, which restricted illegal immigrants' access to social welfare
programs, a newly elected Republican Congress sought to reduce legal
immigration, restrict illegal immigration, and curtail social welfare
benefits for both legal and illegal immigrants. The final version of the
1996 Illegal Immigration Reform and Immigrant Responsibility Act focused on controlling illegal immigration through increased border enforcement and internal enforcement at work sites. In 1996, the Clinton
administration concurred by calling for a greater focus on I-9 reverification checks. Subsequently the INS carried out industry-wide raids of
meat packing plants in Nebraska (Operation Vanguard) and apple or-
chards in Washington. Between the two operations, 3,000 immigrants
were threatened with deportation and fired from their jobs. The 1996

---

[2] Diversity immigrants are nationals of countries with fewer than 50,000 admissions
during the preceding five years. The INS determines country limits on a regional basis
with a maximum per-country diversity visa limit of 3,850 (Department of Justice 2000).

law also intended to discourage future immigration by cutting off benefits for illegal aliens and limiting assistance for legal immigrants.

Despite these efforts to restrict illegal immigration, the number of undocumented immigrants in the United States continues to grow by about 275,000 each year, adding to the estimated 5 million undocu-mented people residing in the country in 1996 (U.S. Department of Jus-tice 2000). For many years, the AFL-CIO supported policies to restrict the number of illegal immigrants, who the union believed were a threat to American workers. "From the perspective of American workers, ille-gal immigration undercuts job opportunities for unemployed Ameri-cans and undermines labor standards for domestic workers"(AFL-CIO 1985, 173). But in the 1990s, the failure of restrictive policies to control illegal immigration and the role these policies played in marginalizing immigrant workers helped bring about a change in the AFL-CIO's stance. Moreover, labor leaders began to see undocumented workers not as a threat to native workers and union activities, but as an impor-tant source of new membership.

The Role of Globalization in Shaping U.S. Labor Leaders' Immigration Preferences

In this country, the restructuring of the world economy has caused a decline in manufacturing jobs and a huge increase in low-paying ser-vice jobs. As corporations move jobs out of the United States seeking the lowest wages and least regulation, standards sink for workers here and abroad. Coming to America seems the only way to create a better life for many people in developing countries. (AFL-CIO 2000a)

Like their European counterparts, American labor union leaders are facing many challenges caused by globalization. As in Spain, Italy, and France, globalization is challenging the U.S. ability to control its bor-ders by making communication and transportation technology more accessible to migrants, and by opening developing countries' economies to greater international trade and capital flows. Globaliza-tion also increases economic competition from low-wage countries, which in turn encourages employers in developed countries to seek out more flexible employment strategies. As a result, the number of contin-

gent jobs has grown at the expense of permanent, full-time employment. This growth of the contingent work force in turn hurts union organizing efforts.

According to the AFL-CIO, contingent or peripheral workers are difficult to organize because of legal impediments imposed by the National Labor Relations Board (NLRB), which presupposes stable employment relationships and a defined bargaining unit for union
organizing drives. Organizing these "orphans of the law," many of
whom are immigrants, is one of the biggest challenges facing unions in
a rapidly changing global economy. As a result, U.S. labor leaders are
devising new strategies to counter the ways globalization disrupts
their recruiting efforts. For example, the AFL-CIO's "Campaign for
Global Fairness" insists that workers' rights be included in all trade
agreements and IMF and World Bank loan agreements (AFL-CIO
2000a).

The AFL-CIO's new immigration platform was developed in the
shadows of global economic changes that have weakened the state's capacity to control its borders, threatened union organization, and marginalized immigrant workers. In this context, the AFL-CIO's starting
points for immigration reform include:

- permanent legal status for undocumented immigrants through a
  new amnesty program;
- eliminating the current system of employer sanctions;
- full workplace rights for immigrant workers;
- cooperative mechanisms between business and labor that allow
  law-abiding employers to satisfy legitimate needs for workers;
- whistle-blower protections for undocumented workers who report
  violations of work protection laws;
- a halt to the expansion of guest worker programs.[3]

On the surface, it appears that globalization is causing U.S. labor
leaders' immigration preferences to converge with those of French, Ital-

---

[3] The AFL-CIO opposes temporary, employment-based immigration, such as the H-
1B program for high-tech specialty occupations; and the H-2B program for skilled or
unskilled seasonal workers. Because temporary immigrants are dependent on their
employers for their visas, the union believes employers use these temporary immigration programs to exploit immigrant and native workers.

ian, and Spanish labor leaders. However, as illustrated in Chapter 3, domestic factors filter the effects of globalization so that labor leaders from different countries, and even different unions in the same country, form different immigration preferences.

One factor unique to the U.S. case is the highly decentralized structure of the AFL-CIO compared to European confederations. The seventy-two national and international unions, not to mention thousands of locals, represented by the administrative umbrella of the AFL-CIO are highly autonomous. As a result, initiatives often originate at the local, regional, or sectoral level and work their way up to the national level. This was the case with immigration reform, which was initiated by four sectoral unions—SEIU, HERE, UFW, and UNITE—beginning in the early 1990s. For each of these unions, immigrants represent an increasingly large segment of their workforce and a promising pool of unorganized labor. The initiative for change also had a regional dimension. In 1994, two California regional labor confederations, Alameda and Los Angeles, called for an end to employer sanctions and a new amnesty for undocumented workers. These demands gradually worked their way up to the national level of the AFL-CIO, and were facilitated by a new leadership team elected in 1995 that was open to change and intent on increasing union membership.

This "trickle-up" effect stands in contrast to the top-down structure of more centralized European unions. In Spain, Italy, and France, changes in labor leaders' immigration preferences occurred first among the top leadership, at the confederal level, and worked its way down to regional and sectoral unions through educational initiatives for the rank and file, and through local provision of social and legal services for immigrant workers.

Below I discuss three factors that have helped shape U.S. labor leaders' immigration preferences: the failure of government sanctions to reduce employer demand for illegal immigrant workers, declining union membership rates and the resultant emphasis on organizing, and the exploitation of immigrant workers on the margins of the labor market.

The Failure of Employer Sanctions

Current efforts to improve immigration enforcement, while failing to stop the flow of undocumented people into the United States, have resulted in a system that causes discrimination and leaves unpunished unscrupulous employers who exploit undocumented workers, thus denying labor rights for all workers. (AFL-CIO 2000c)

Central to the AFL-CIO's new immigration position is the belief that the current system of immigration enforcement is "broken and needs to be fixed." The AFL-CIO immigration reform program highlights several problems with U.S. law, such as flawed guest worker programs, delays in the naturalization process, and the failure to legalize thousands of undocumented immigrants who were eligible for the 1986 amnesty. However, the AFL-CIO believes the most egregious flaw in U.S. immigration policy is the failure of employer sanctions to reduce employer demand for illegal immigrant workers.

In the 1980s, the AFL-CIO supported sanctions against employers who hired undocumented immigrants. The leadership believed that sanctions would protect American jobs by discouraging employers from hiring cheap, illegal immigrant labor. They also believed that sanctions would help reduce illegal immigration by cutting off the demand for foreign labor. With the backing of labor unions, employer sanctions became a pillar of the 1986 Immigration Reform and Control Act. However, as mentioned previously, policy-makers lacked the political will to give teeth to the enforcement provision of IRCA. As a result, the INS did not have the legal or physical capacity to enforce employer sanctions successfully.

Not surprisingly, then, the employer sanctions provision of IRCA has not arrested the demand for, or supply of, illegal immigrants. In fact, after falling to between 1.8 and 3 million people after 1986, the undocumented population rose to between 2.7 and 3.7 million by 1992. Nor have unsystematically enforced sanctions discouraged employers from hiring illegal immigrants. In fact, according to many labor leaders, rather than protecting the employment rights of native and legal immigrant workers, employer sanctions have been turned against workers. "On the surface this [IRCA] looks like an anti-employer law. In reality it's an anti-worker law"(Labor Immigrant Organizers Network 1999).

For example, labor leaders are concerned with how employers use I-9 audits to threaten immigrant workers. In one case, a manager of a Holiday Inn Express in Minneapolis called into his office eight undocumented employees who recently had voted for representation with

HERE. The workers were met by INS officials and arrested. The manager said he called the INS because he feared he would be penalized for knowingly hiring undocumented workers. But many labor leaders have a different view. They argue that employers are using I-9 audits to frighten immigrant workers and discourage union organizing drives. "Immigration law is a tool of the employers," to Cristina Vasquez, Los Angeles Regional Manager for UNITE. "They're able to use it as a weapon to keep workers unorganized, and the INS has helped them"(Bacon 1999). By the early 1990s, labor leaders in sectors and regions with a high concentration of immigrant workers were losing confidence in the state's ability to enforce fair and effective employer sanctions.

In the February 2000 resolution, the AFL-CIO called for eliminating the current I-9 system as a tool for workplace immigration enforcement. In its place, the organization wants a policy that penalizes employers who recruit undocumented workers from abroad and gives illegal immigrant workers whistle-blower protections for reporting violations.

Immigrants as a Potential Pool of New Union Members

The change in U.S. labor leaders' immigration preferences has been heavily influenced by the desire to build union membership, which has declined steadily since the 1950s. After reaching a peak of about 35 percent of the workforce in 1953, by the late 1990s union density rates declined overall to less than 15 percent, and to about 10 percent in the private sector (Nissen 1999; Milkman 2000).

Many labor leaders, including former AFL-CIO President Lane Kirkland, were complacent about this loss of membership. In the early 1990s, in fact, President Kirkland was quoted as saying, "We've maintained our membership in the most extraordinary combination of adverse circumstances" (1999, 11).

But in the United States, where membership dictates union bargaining power with employers, the AFL-CIO does not enjoy an institutionalized role in collective bargaining at the national or sectoral level, as unions often do in Europe. Likewise, U.S. collective bargaining agreements do not cover workers who are not members in a union. Therefore, in contrast to their European counterparts, American labor leaders increasingly see immigrant workers as a crucial source of new membership to bolster union strength.

In the first contested election in AFL-CIO history, John Sweeney and his team won the 1995 elections with a campaign to revitalize the labor movement by increasing union membership and political clout. In his inaugural address to the AFL-CIO, Sweeney promised to devote more manpower and money to organizing efforts.

The AFL-CIO's new leadership team includes Sweeney, the son of Irish immigrants; Linda Chavez-Thompson, the granddaughter of Mexican immigrants; and Richard Trumka, from a family of Polish and Italian immigrants. Not surprisingly, this group quickly recognized that immigrant workers would be an important component of the AFL-CIO's efforts to increase union membership. However, several structural and legal obstacles stood in the way of organizing immigrant workers through traditional strategies.

Beginning in the 1970s and 1980s, economic restructuring forced new immigrants, many of them undocumented, into peripheral jobs that lacked union representation. For example, in the 1990s foreign-born Latinos made up about 17 percent of California's total workforce, but they constituted 36 percent of its service workers and 49 percent of its laborers (Milkman 2000, 11). Because immigrant workers tend to be concentrated in the unskilled, contingent workforce, legal barriers imposed by the NLRB make traditional organizing efforts difficult. As a result, immigrant workers and local unions have circumvented the NLRB and devised new organizing strategies. Many of these strategies are explored in Ruth Milkman, *Organizing Immigrants* (2000), Bruce Nissen *Which Direction for Organized Labor?* (1999), and Kate Bronfenbrenner et al. *Organizing to Win* (1998).

Also standing in the way of immigrant unionization is the fear of employer retaliation. One of the eight employees of the Holiday Inn Express in Minneapolis who voted for union representation in HERE expressed this fear at an AFL-CIO immigration town hall meeting. "A week before negotiations started, management turned us into the INS in retaliation for organizing a union" (AFL-CIO 2000b, 8). And, as mentioned previously, some employers have used the I-9 reverification process as a means to discourage union organizing efforts. "Employers have systematically used the I-9 process in their efforts to retaliate against workers who seek to join unions, improve their working conditions and otherwise assert their rights"(AFL-CIO 2000c).

The AFL-CIO wants to remove these barriers. First, labor leaders argue that the fear of employer retaliation must be eliminated by legalizing undocumented workers and granting immigrants and natives equal workplace rights. Second, they say that the current I-9 system of employer sanctions must end. Finally, labor leaders want whistleblower protections for undocumented immigrants who report employer violations. According to AFL-CIO Executive Vice President Linda Chavez-Thompson, "Too often, immigrant workers' rights are being routinely violated. Courageous undocumented workers who come forward to assert their rights should not be faced with deportation as a result of their actions"(AFL-CIO 2000b).

Exploitation of Immigrant Workers on the Margins of the Labor Market

Economic marginalization of undocumented immigrants is a recurring theme in the AFL-CIO's immigration reform dialogue. According to one of the organization's associate general counsels, "It serves no one's interest to have an exploitable work force. Undocumented workers who are exploited are less willing to complain about abuses, so everyone suffers"(Burns 2000).

However, U.S. labor leaders do not equate illegal immigration with the growth of the underground economy, nor do they see legalization as a means to shrink the underground economy. In contrast to Spain and Italy, where underground economic activity makes up between 20 to 25 percent of GDP, in the United States the underground economy is significantly smaller at about 8 percent of GDP (Schneider and Enste 2000).

American labor leaders also differ from their French counterparts, who support amnesty only on humanitarian grounds. U.S. labor leaders support amnesty for other reasons. First, granting permanent residency status to undocumented immigrants will allow them to achieve stability in the workplace, which the unions believe will ultimately benefit all workers. "The depth and the breadth of immigrant exploitation by employers means that all workers are at risk"(author interview,

Matt Finucane, Associate General Counsel, AFL-CIO, May 2000). Second, many labor leaders believe that granting amnesty is a means to increase union membership. According to Eliseo Medina, executive vice president with the Los Angeles–based SEIU, the goal of the AFL-CIO's new immigration policy is to boost membership by offering union support to the labor force's least powerful segment (Lindquist 2000).

Like their Spanish, Italian, and French counterparts, labor leaders in the United States favor more open immigration policies and believe that restrictive policies fail to control illegal immigration. What's more, they have resigned themselves to the fact that regulated legal immigration is better than unregulated illegal immigration. However, they reached these conclusions in different ways, ways that depend largely on the domestic pressures they are subject to. U.S. labor leaders place more emphasis on increasing union membership. Hence, they support legalization and an end to employer sanctions as a means to reduce the risk of immigrant-organizing drives.

In Spain, Italy and France, unions have acted on their immigration preferences and helped moderate immigration policies. Whether U.S. labor leaders are able to achieve a similarly proactive policy agenda remains to be seen. However, the convergence of labor leaders' and employers' immigration preferences offers a unique opportunity to shape policy.

Explaining U.S. Employers' Pro-Immigration Policy Preferences

Changes in the global economy have helped shape the immigration policy preferences of French, Spanish, Italian and U.S. employers. In Europe and the United States, employers, in response to increasing global economic competition, have discarded mass production models in favor of flexible and decentralized production and employment strategies, such as subcontracting, relocating production overseas, and temporary and part-time contracts. Likewise, global economic restructuring has encouraged a bifurcation of the labor market between highly skilled, information-based workers and low-skilled workers. Employers in the United States and Europe increasingly are looking abroad to recruit both skilled technology workers and unskilled workers.

In contrast to European national employers' associations, many U.S. employers are openly pro-immigration. Most American employers, from growers to software manufacturers to restaurant owners, want more permanent and temporary employment-based immigration. Some even favor an amnesty for undocumented workers. For example, the Essential Workers Immigration Coalition, a group of businesses and trade associations concerned with a shortage of semi-skilled and unskilled workers, wants undocumented immigrants who have been working in the United States to be allowed to legalize their status (EWIC 2000).

One explanation for the differing attitudes of European and American employers is economic. The more flexible U.S. economy did not suffer as deep or as long an economic recession as Europe did after the 1973 oil crisis, so that employer demand for immigrant workers has been more prevalent and politically palatable in the United States However, I believe other explanations beyond economic cycles of growth and recession, such as differences in the policy-making process and the decentralization of business interests in the United States, help explain U.S. employers' openly pro-immigration policy preferences.

The Immigration Policy-Making Process in the United States

The American immigration policy-making process is fundamentally different from that in Europe. This is in part because for historical and cultural reasons the United States considers itself to be a "country of immigration," whereas Spain, Italy, and France do not. As a result, immigration policy debates in the United States almost always include discussion on whether to decrease, maintain, or increase annual immigration quotas. Even in the mid-1990s, when the public debate shifted to the provision of social welfare benefits for legal and illegal immigrants, the "appropriate" level of legal immigration was debated in Congress. During these debates, employers responded to threats of restricting skill-based immigration by successfully lobbying to kill portions of bills that sought to reduce legal immigration.

Also, the politicization of U.S. immigration policy is bound to the perceived social and economic costs of illegal immigration. Employers, who want access to immigrant labor, have therefore pursued a clever lobbying strategy of splitting the legal and illegal components of immigration bills. For example, an early Senate version of the 1996 Illegal Immigration Reform and Immigrant Responsibility Act included a measure to reduce skill-based visas from 140,000 to 90,000. Many employers and employer groups, including the National Association of Manufacturers, Microsoft, and the U.S. Chamber of Commerce, were outraged by these proposals (Lee 1998, 109). Business lobbyists mobilized to "split the bill" between its legal and illegal components, thereby maintaining legal immigration levels. This strategy, also pursued by employers with the 1990 Immigration Act, allows government to ease public concerns about illegal immigration by fortifying borders or restricting access to social services. At the same time, legislators can satisfy employer demand for immigrant labor by maintaining or increasing legal immigration levels.

Since France, Italy, and Spain are not "countries of immigration," the politics of immigration policy often hinges less on numbers and more on how to integrate different immigrant populations ethnically, culturally, and linguistically. Most European employers do not see immigrant integration as a "company" concern, and the politically charged debates over models of immigrant incorporation discourage European employers from entering the policy-making process.

The Decentralized Organization of U.S. Business Interests

Unlike most European employers, who belong to national employers' organizations that speak on their behalf, U.S. employers largely operate as free agents in their efforts to influence the immigration policy-making process. When interests converge among individual employers, such as growers or computer and software manufacturers, they may form politically powerful lobbying groups that work with members of Congress to develop industry-specific immigration policy.

The most experienced industry group in lobbying for employment-based immigration is agribusiness. This sector has received special treatment in immigration matters because American agriculture is considered an economic success story for its ability to provide low-cost food and generate a consistent trade surplus. And the success of U.S. agriculture is closely linked to Mexican immigration. For example, nearly two-thirds of the workers who farm the fruit, nuts, vegetables, and horticultural specialties are immigrants (Martin 1998).

In 1917, growers used the slogan "Food to Win the War" to persuade the U.S. Department of Labor to suspend the head tax and literacy tests for Mexican workers coming to the United States with contracts less than twelve months long. This first "Bracero Program" paved the way for a much larger Bracero Program that brought some 4.6 million Mexicans to work on U.S. farms between 1942 and 1964 (Martin 2000, 1).

Since the end of the Bracero Program in the mid-1960s, growers have been lobbying for an alternative guest worker program. In the 1980s, growers launched a well-financed campaign to defeat employer sanctions and to broaden the H-2 program for temporary agricultural workers against heavy opposition from labor and civil rights groups. As a result, the 1986 IRCA included a two-year exemption from employer sanctions for growers and two new seasonal guest worker programs, the H-2A program and the Replenishment Agricultural Worker (RAW) program. More recently, agricultural employers have backed several bills (HR.4548, HR.4056, S.1814, and S.1815) that would allow undocumented workers to legalize their status if they can prove they did at least 150 days of farm work in the previous year. These workers could then become permanent residents if they performed at least 180 days of farm work each year for five of the next seven years.

A more recent entrant into the immigration policy-making process has been the high-tech industry. Beginning in the 1990s, high-tech companies devoted considerable resources to lobbying for increases in the H-1B visa program, which brings temporary skilled immigrant labor to the United States For example, the Center for Responsive Politics, a nonpartisan, nonprofit research group, reported that computer and Internet companies donated $8,891,792 in political action committee, soft money, and individual contributions during the 1995–1996 election cycle. This was 46 percent more than was spent in the 1991–1992 election cycle. Preliminary reports for the 2000 election cycle show the computer and Internet industry donated $38,941,626 to federal candidates and political parties (Center for Responsive Politics 2001). Individual employers such as Microsoft, Intel, Cisco, Amazon.com, Texas Instruments, and Oracle have been at the forefront of lobbying efforts, and have been aided by industry employer organizations, including the Information Technology Association of America (ITAA), the American Electronics Association (AEA) and the Semiconductor Industry Association (SIA). These industry groups commissioned various studies that demonstrated a shortage of high-tech workers, provided hours of congressional testimony, and gave considerable campaign donations to members of Congress.

Despite inconclusive evidence of a long-term shortage of high-tech workers, the industry was successful in its efforts to raise the annual H-1B visa cap from 65,000 to 115,000 under the 1998 American Competitiveness Workforce Improvement Act. Two years later, the cap was raised again, to 195,000 under the 2000 American Competitiveness in the Twenty-First Century Act.

Following the lead of high-tech companies, employers concerned with the shortage of "essential"(semi-skilled and low-skilled) workers formed their own lobbying group in 1999. Members of EWIC include the American Health Care Association, the American Hotel and Motel Association, the American Meat Institute, the Associated Builders and Contractors, the National Retail Federation, the National Restaurant Association, and the U.S. Chamber of Commerce. EWIC members believe that current immigration law has curtailed the source of essential workers. Their reform agenda includes:

- New legal immigration programs based on worker shortages, such as an effective temporary employment-based immigration program and employment-based permanent residence for essential workers;
- Legalization of certain undocumented workers through a one-time, employment-contingent amnesty;
- Workable immigration enforcement, including a repeal of the current employer sanctions system.

In 2000, EWIC began to make its case to Congress for an increase in semi-and low-skilled immigration through various lobbying efforts, including letter writing campaigns and congressional testimony. EWIC hopes that the legislative success of the high-tech lobby in increasing the number of skilled immigrant visas will carry over into more semi-and low-skilled immigration (author interview, John Gay, Co-Chair, EWIC, October 2000).

These well-funded, intensive congressional lobbying efforts by companies and industry-specific employer groups to win increases in immigration quotas stand in sharp contrast to the more low-key, bureaucratic approach of European employers' associations to develop national immigration quotas. European and U.S. employers share the basic belief that they should be free to hire the most qualified worker regardless of his or her country of origin. However, how European and American employers act on their preferences for open immigration policies differs dramatically. In the United States, the policy-making process lends itself to active employer involvement by focusing on numbers and industry-specific legislation. On the other hand, national European employers' associations have taken a back seat in the policy-making process claiming that immigration policy does not address "company" concerns.

Prospects for U.S. Business and Labor Influence on the Immigration Policy-Making Process

Labor and business should work together to design cooperative mechanisms that allow law-abiding employers to satisfy legitimate needs for new workers in a timely manner without compromising the rights and opportunities of workers already here. (AFL-CIO 2000c)

The AFL-CIO's new immigration stance opens the door for cooperation between employers and unions on immigration policy. (Author interview, John Gay, Co-Chair, EWIC, October 2000)

Will the AFL-CIO be able to shape the immigration policy-making process to meet its immigration reform agenda? Several indicators suggest that the AFL-CIO has a window of opportunity to do exactly that. First, the low unemployment and high economic growth rates of the late 1990s have created a more immigrant-friendly political environment than existed in the mid 1990s. For example, in 2000 there was little opposition to increasing the number of visas for highly skilled workers. Second, the emphasis that AFL-CIO President John Sweeney has placed on improving the union's political clout through campaign donations, get-out-the-vote drives, and organizing initiatives should help to place immigration reform on the political agenda of Democratic members of Congress. Third, and most important, the AFL-CIO has powerful pro-immigration allies in business and immigrant advocacy groups.

The AFL-CIO already has capitalized on connections with Latino and Asian community groups and immigrant organizations, who have common interests in legalizing undocumented immigrants and improving workplace rights for immigrants. At the grassroots level, local unions and immigrant rights advocates are building labor and community alliances to support immigrant workers' rights. For instance, the Los Angeles Federation of Labor has hosted meetings between local unions and immigrant rights advocates, such as the Korean Immigrant Workers Association, the Coalition for Humane Immigrant Rights of Los Angeles, and the One Stop Immigration and Education Center. At the national level, information and political strategies are shared between the AFL-CIO and immigrant advocacy groups such as the National Network for Immigrant and Refugee Rights, the National Council of La Raza, the National Korean American Service and Education Consortium, the National Immigration Law Center, the Asian Pacific American Labor Alliance, and the League of United Latin American Citizens. However, to build a broader cross-party alliance, the AFL-CIO must take advantage of the convergence of its immigration interests with those of employers.

Business and labor find common ground in the need for an amnesty, an end to employer sanctions, and legal mechanisms that allow employers to satisfy legitimate needs for immigrant workers. Of course business and labor have reached this common ground by different routes. Employers want access to a larger pool of labor and fewer restrictions on their ability to recruit and hire immigrant workers. Labor wants to level the playing field between immigrant workers and employers, and to organize immigrant workers into unions. What's more, business and labor still disagree on temporary or guest worker immigration programs. Employers support temporary immigration programs as a way to satisfy short-term demand for immigrant labor. But unions believe guest worker programs are often used by employers to discriminate against American workers, and create a class of easily exploitable immigrant workers by tying immigrants to a specific employer and period of employment. Nevertheless, a powerful left-right political alliance could emerge from this unique and timely convergence of immigration interests.

Such an alliance started to unfold in the spring of 2000 during two meetings of business and labor leaders to discuss immigration reform. The meetings were convened by Jack Kemp, former Republican vice-presidential candidate and secretary of Housing and Urban Development for the Reagan administration, and Henry Cisneros, former secretary of Housing and Urban Development for the Clinton administration. Their purpose was to build a broad-based coalition that would lobby Congress to admit more legal immigrants and grant amnesty to more than 400,000 undocumented immigrants.

Both labor and business leaders came away from the meetings hopeful that cooperation would continue and that business and labor ultimately could achieve some of their mutual policy goals. Eliseo Medina, Executive Vice President of the Service Employees International Union, called the meetings a good first step because they brought together a widely disparate group of employers and unions, political conservatives, and immigrant rights advocates. Likewise, John Wilhelm, president of the Hotel Employees and Restaurant Employees International Union, urged, "this is the time to be bold. In the legislative process we'll wind up bargaining and what we get will depend on how strong our coalition is"(Bacon 2000). And John Gay, co-chair of EWIC, believes that the door is now open for cooperation with unions (author interview, October 2000).

One indicator of the potential for cooperation between business and labor is their mutual support of the 2000 Latino and Immigrant Fairness Act (S.2912). The bill is backed by the AFL-CIO as well as various employer groups including the U.S. Chamber of Commerce, the American Health Care Association, the American Hotel and Motel Association, the American Nursing Association, the American Nursery and Landscaping Association, Associated Builders and Contractors, and the Associated General Contractors. If passed, the act would allow hundreds of thousands of undocumented immigrants who have been residing in the United States since before 1986 to legalize their status. It would grant permanent asylum to about 300,000 undocumented immigrants who fled civil wars and political chaos in El Salvador,

Guatemala, Honduras, Haiti, and Liberia during the 1980s and 1990s. Finally, the act would restore provision 245(i), which allows undocumented immigrants with family or employer ties to remain in the United States while waiting for their visas, rather than having to return to their country of origin.

The Latino and Immigrant Fairness Act is opposed by many Republican members of Congress, who believe that a new amnesty would encourage more illegal immigration. In an attempt to compromise with pro-immigrant forces, Republicans proposed alternative legislation that grants special temporary visas to spouses and minor children of permanent residents who have waited for more than three years for green cards to become available. Their proposal also allows some 400,000 immigrants who missed the IRCA application deadline to legalize their status. This compromise legislation was passed days before the 106th Congress adjourned in December 2000.

Because many Republicans and Democrats in Congress remain divided on immigration, business and labor will have to work together to lobby effectively for broader reforms such as a general amnesty, a new employer sanctions system, and new mechanisms for temporary legal immigration.

Conclusion

In the United States, as in Europe, employers and labor union leaders—former adversaries in the debate over immigration policy—have come to accept the realities of globalization. Faced with increasing wage and price competition from developing countries, many employers in the United States, Spain, Italy, and France are experimenting with more flexible employment strategies, such as subcontracting and temporary contracts, and hiring cheap immigrant workers where possible. Labor unions, for their part, have broadened their organizing strategies to encompass the growing number of peripheral workers, many of them immigrants, that is replacing their core membership.

Beyond the state, labor unions and employers are developing new organizations and relationships to deal with global and regional changes. Through the European Trade Union Confederation, for example, labor leaders are sharing information and political strategies and pooling resources to influence immigration policy at the European Union level. And as a result of the North American Free Trade Agreement, labor leaders from the United States and Mexico are building cross-border ties in an effort to improve working conditions and wages among Mexican workers. Meanwhile, businesses are consolidating through international partnerships and moving some production abroad to low-wage countries.

Politically, globalization has had a peculiar effect on labor leaders' immigration views, causing the preferences of unions and employers to converge around more open policies. For many labor leaders, more legal and illegal immigration is an inevitable consequence of globalization. The restrictive immigration policies of the 1970s and 1980s not only failed to stop immigration, they forced many immigrants into a precarious economic position. Unable to protect their core constituency from an influx of cheap immigrant labor, most labor leaders have rejected restrictive policies in favor of measures that promote legal immigration.

Yet despite the important role that globalization plays in shaping preferences and policy outcomes, the strategies that labor leaders and employers use to confront global economic changes are diverse because they are influenced by varying domestic factors. Domestic circumstances—such as the prevalence of underground employment—help explain why Spanish and Italian labor leaders support temporary, employment-based quotas, while U.S. and French labor leaders oppose similar guest worker programs. They also shed light on why employers, who share a fundamental desire to hire the most qualified workers regardless of their country of origin, have different strategies for influencing the immigration policy-making process. As U.S. labor leaders enter the immigration policy-making process, they would be wise to remain cognizant of these domestic factors and learn from the experiences of their French, Spanish, and Italian colleagues how to best achieve their reform agenda.

Bibliography

ACLP World Political/Economic Database. 1995. M. Alvarez, J. A. Cheibub, F. Limongi, and A. Przeworski.

AFL-CIO 1985. "Immigration Reform." 16th National Convention of the AFL-CIO. Anaheim, Calif. October 28.

AFL-CIO 2000a. "Recognizing Our Common Bonds." *America@work*, October 2000 (a monthly AFL-CIO magazine).

AFL-CIO 2000b. "Building Understanding—Creating Change." A report that can be obtained from the AFL-CIO.

AFL-CIO 2000c. "Immigration." Executive Council Statement. February 16.

Aizpeolea, L. 1999. "El Gobierno Bloqueará en el Senado la Ley de Extranjería con las Enmiendas de Interior." *El Pais*, November 20.

Appelbaum, E., and R. Batt. 1994. *The New American Workplace: Transforming Work Systems in the United States*. Ithaca, N.Y.: ILR Press.

Aragón Bombin, R. 1996. "Diez Años de Politica de Inmigración." *Migraciones* 1:45–59.

Aragón Bombin, R., and J. C. Pedrero. 1993. *La Regularización de Inmigrantes durante 1991–1992*. Madrid: Ministerio de Trabajo y Seguridad Social.

Associazione Nazionale oltre le Frontiere. 1997. "2nd Assemblea Nazionale: Immigrati Ricchezza per la Societa e Protagonisti nella CISL." Rome. January 23.

Bacon, D. 1999. "Immigrant Workers: The Law that Keeps Them Chained." *LA Weekly*, October 8–14.

Baggaley, J. 1998. "Moroccans shrug off death at sea, flock to Europe." *Reuters*, March 17.

Baglioni, G., and C. Crouch, eds. 1990. *European Industrial Relations: The Challenge of Flexibility*. London: Sage.

Baldwin-Edwards, M. 1991. "Immigration after 1992." *Policy and Politics* 19(3):199–211.

Baldwin-Edwards, M., and M. Schain. 1994. *The Politics of Immigration in Western Europe*. New York: Frank Cass.

Bayade, F., A. Labrousse, and M-C. Héléna. Direction de la Population et des Migrations. 1995. "L'Insertion Professionnelle des Etrangers, 1990–1994." Ministere de L'Integration et de la Lutte contre l'exclusion, Notes et Documents, no. 23, October 1995.

Bedani, G. 1995. *Politics and Ideology in the Italian Workers' Movement*. Providence, R.I.: Berg.

Berger, S., and R. Dore, eds. 1996. *National Diversity and Global Capitalism*. Ithaca, N.Y.: Cornell University Press.

Berger, S., and M. J. Piore 1980. *Dualism and Discontinuity in Industrial Society*. Cambridge: Cambridge University Press.

Best, M. 1990. *The New Competition: Institutions of Industrial Restructuring*. Cambridge: Harvard University Press.

Blanco Fdez. De Valderrama, C. 1993. "The New Hosts: The Case of Spain." *International Migration Review* 27(1):169–81.

Boletin Oficial de las Cortes Generales. 1985. "Ley Organica 7/1985, sobre Derechos y Libertades de los Extranjeros en España." July 3.

——. 1991. "Proposiciones no de Ley Ante el Pleno." March 22.

——. 1996. Real Decreto 155/1996. February 2.

Borras, A., ed. 1995. *Diez Años de la Ley de Extranjería: Balance y Perspectivas*. Barcelona: Fundación Paulino Torras Doménech.

Brochmann, G. 1996. *European Integration and Immigration from Third Countries*. Oslo: Scandinavian University Press.

Bronfenbrenner, K., S. Friedman, R. W. Hurd, R. A. Oswald, and R. L. Seeber, eds. 1998. *Organizing to Win*. Ithaca, N.Y.: Cornell University Press.

Burns, T. 2000. "Unions Halt Decline in Membership." *Washington Times*, January 10.

Cachón Rodriguez, L. 1993. "Informe sobre la Inmigración en España." Geneva: ILO.

——. 1995. "Marco Institucional de la Discriminación y Tipos de Inmigrante en el Mercado de Trabajo en España." *Revista Española de Investigaciones Sociologicas* 69:105–24.

——. 1997. "Case Study on the Prevention of Racial Discrimination and Xenophobia and the Promotion of Equal Treatment in the Workplace, Spain." Working Paper No. WP/97/46. Dublin: European Foundation for the Improvement of Living and Working Conditions.

Calavita, K. 1997. "Immigration, Law and Marginalization in a Global Economy: Notes from Spain." Unpublished manuscript. University of California, Irvine: Dept. of Criminolgy, Law, and Society.

——. 1998. "Gaps and Contradictions in U.S. Immigration Policy." In *The Immigration Reader*, edited by D. Jacobsen. Malden, Mass.: Blackwell.

Callovi, G. 1992. "Regulation of Immigration in 1993: Pieces of the European Jigsaw Puzzle." *International Migration Review* 26(2):353–72.

Caritas di Roma. 1997. *Immigrazione Dossier Statistico*. Rome: Anterem.

——. 1999. *Immigrazione Dossier Statistico*. Rome: Anterem

Casey, J. 1998. "La Inmigración Extranjera: Un ambito emergente de políticas." In *Políticas Públicas en España*, edited by J. Subirats and R. Goma. Madrid: Ariel.

Castles, S., and Kosack, G. 1973. *Immigrant Workers and Class Structure in Western Europe*. London: Billing and Sons.

CCOO. 1994. "Jornada de Movilización por la Reforma del Reglamento Extranjeria." *Cuadernos de Migraciones*. November 1994.

——. 1995a. Centre de Información para Trabajadores Extranjeros. *Recull Anual sobre Inmigración*.

——. 1995b. Secretaría Confederal de Migraciones. "Dossier de Prensa: Reforma del Reglamento y su Aprobación." (Press packet)

——. 1996a. Secretaría Confederal de Migraciones. Dossier de Prensa: Reforma del Reglamento y su Aprobación. 1996a. "CCOO y UGT Piden a Gonzalez que se Apruebe el Reglamento de Extranjeria." January 31.

——. 1996b. Secretaría Condederal de Migraciones. "Dossier de Prensa: Proceso de Documentación, 23/4/96–23/08/96." (Press packet)

——. 1996c. "Somos Diferentes, Somos Iguales: Trabajadores más allá de las Fronteras." Centro de Información para Trabajadores Migrantes. (Pamphlet)

——. 1996d. "CCOO Inicia una Gran Campana de Información y Regularización: Entra en Vigor un Nuevo Regalmento de Extranjeria." *Gaceta Sindical*, April, p. 39.

——. 1997a. "Propuesta Sobrenlas Oficinas Únicas de Extranjeros." October. (Proposal made by CCOO to government)

——. 1997b. Secretaría de Acción Social y Migraciones. "Jornadas Andaluzas sobre Migraciones." October.

CENSIS. 1997. *Rapporto sulla Situazione Sociale del Paese*. Rome: Francoangeli.

Center for Responsive Politics. 2002. www.opensecrets.org.

Centro de Investigaciones Sociológicas. 1996. "Atitudes ante la Inmigración." Estudio 2.214, (survey) June.

CFDT. 1997. "L'Immigration: Réalité Incontournable d"un Monde Qui Bouge." (Union pamphlet)

CGIL. 1993. Coordinamento Nazionale Immigrati. 1st Assemblea Nazionale. "Parita di diritti e solidarieta tra diversi." (Proposals for immigration reform)

——. 1994. Coordinamento Nazionale Immigrati. "Rappresentanza Sindacale e Cittadinanza Sociale." 2nd Assemblea Nazionale. Naples, November 25–26.

——. 1996a. Dipartimento Politiche Attiva del Lavoro. "La CGIL e l'Immigrazione." Quaderno no. 10.

——. 1996b. Dipartimento Politiche Attiva del Lavoro. "All Different All Equal." Quaderno no. 11.

——. 1996c. Coordinamento Nazionale Immigrati. "Lavoro e Non Solo." Supplemento a Nuova Rassegna Sindeicale. (Union publication)

——. 1997. "Disegno di Legge sull'Immigrazione." (Handout of union statement on text of immigration law passed by Chamber of Deputies on 11/19/97)

CGT. 1997a. "Memoire en Matière d"Immigration." (Handout)

——. 1997b. "Declaration de la CGT: Une veritable regularisation doit être engagée." (Union statement on Pasqua and Debré laws and immigration reform)

———. 1997c. "Le Racisme hors de la Loi: Campagne de la CGT contre le Racisme et pour le Fraternité." (Handout on CGTs Tour de France)

Chemouil, G. 1997. "Reaggissons face au racisme." *Tribune de l'Immigration* 21:4–5.

Cheng, L., and E. Bonacich. 1984. *Labor Immigration under Capitalism: Asian Workers in the United States before World War II*. Berkeley: University of California Press.

Chiswick, B. R. 1988. "Illegal Immigration and Immigration Control." *Journal of Economic Perspectives* 2(3):101–15.

Christensen, D. 1997. "Leaving the Backdoor Open: Italy's Response to Illegal Immigration." *Georgetown University Law Journal* 11(3):461–505.

CISL. 1997a. "Cos'é la CISL." Rome: Edizioni Lavoro Roma. (Booklet on history, politics, and organization of CISL)

———. 1997b. "Impariamo l'Uguaglianza: Contro Ogni Rassa di Razzismo." (Handout)

Colectivo Ioé. 1991. "Trabajadoras Extranjeras de Servicio Doméstico en Madrid, España." Working Paper. Madrid: Colectivo Ioé.

———. 1996. "Actividades de Formación Antidiscriminatoria en España." Informe Ocasional. Geneva: Departamento de Empleo y Formación.

Collinson, S. 1994. "Toward Further Harmonization? Migration Policy in the European Union." *Studi Emigrazione* 31(14):210–37.

Cornelius, W., P. Martin, and J. Hollifield, eds. 1994. *Controlling Immigration: A Global Perspective*. Stanford: Stanford University Press.

Crouch, C., and G. Baglioni, eds. 1990. *European Industrial Relations: The Challenge of Flexibility*. London: Sage.

Crouch, C., and F. Traxler. 1995. *Organized Industrial Relations in Europe: What Future?* Brookfield, Vt.: Ashgate.

Cruz, A. 1999. "Achievements in the Fields of Immigration and Asylum since January 1998." *European Journal of Migration and Law* 1:243–54.

Dallago, B. 1990. *The Irregular Economy*. Brookfield, Vt.: Gower.

Debs, E. 1910. "A Letter on Immigration" *International Socialist Review* 10:16–17.

Dell'Aringa, C., and F. Neri. 1987. "Illegal Immigrants and the Informal Economy in Italy." *Labour* 1:107–26.

DeRudder, V., C. Poiret, and F. Vourc'h. 1997. "Case Study on the Prevention of Racial Discrimination and Xenophobia and the Promotion of Equal Treatment in the Workplace, France." Working Paper No. WP/97/38. Dublin: European Foundation for the Improvement of Living and Working Conditions.

Djajic S. 1997. "Illegal Immigration and Resource Allocation." *International Economic Review* 38:97–177.

Economic and Social Research Institute. 1997. "Case Studies of Good Practices for the Prevention of Racial Discrimination and Xenophobia and the Promotion of Equal Treatment in the Workplace." Working Paper WP/97/42/EN. Dublin: European Foundation for the Improvement of Living and Working Conditions.

Economist. 1997. "A Light on the Shadows." April 3, p. 63.

El Pais. 1996. "CCOO y UGT Piden a Gonzalez que se Apruebe el Reglamento de Extranjeria." January 31.

European Commission. 2000. "Asylum and Immigration Debate." IP/00/1340. Brussels. November 22.

European Council. 1997. "Presidency Conclusions." Amsterdam. June 16–17.

———. 1999. "Presidency Press Conference." Tampere, Finland. October 16.

EWIC. 2000. "Immigration Reform Agenda." www.ewic.com.

Fassmann, H., and R. Munz, eds. 1994. *European Migration in the Late Twentieth Century*. Brookfield, Vt.: Edward Elgar.

Faye, A. B. 2000. "Unionism and Immigration in Italy." Paper presented at the In Migration Conference, Claremont, Calif. March.

Ferner, A., and R. Hyman, eds. 1992. *Industrial Relations in the New Europe*. Oxford: Blackwell.

Foro para la Integración Social de los Inmigrantes. 1997. "Informe sobre la Inmigración y el Asilo en España." October 22.

Freeman, G. 1978. "Immigrant Labor and Working Class Politics: The French and British Experience." *Comparative Politics* Vol. II (October): pp. 24–41.

Frieden, J., and R. Rogowski. 1998. "The Impact of International Economy on National Policies: An Analytic Overview." In *Internationalization and Domestic Politics*, edited by R. Keohane and H. Milner. New York: Cambridge University Press.

Fundación Iberoamerica-Europa Centro de Investigaciones, Promociones y Cooperación Internacional. 1996, 1997, 1998. "Analisis de Prensa sobre Inmigración." (Collection of news articles)

Garrett, G., and P. Lange. 1995. "Internationalization, Institutions and Political Change." *International Organization* 49(4):627–55.

Gazzetta Ufficiale della Repubblica Italiana. 1998. "Disciplina dell'immigrazione e norme sulla condizione dello staniero." Rome. March 12.

Golden, M. 1997. "Economic Integration and Industrial Relations: Is Increasing Economic Openness Bad for Labor?" Paper presented at the American Political Science Association Annual Meeting, Washington, D.C. August.

Golden, M., M. Wallerstein, and P. Lange. 1998. "Union Centralization among Advanced Industrial Societies." Electronic data set available at http://emma.sscnet.ucla.edu/data/

Gompers, S. 1911. "Immigration—Up to Congress." *American Federationist* 13(1): 17–21.

Haas, E. 1958. *The Uniting of Europe: Political, Economic, and Social Forces, 1950–1957*. Stanford: Stanford University Press.

Hall, P. 1986. *Governing the Economy*. New York: Oxford University Press.

Haus, L. 1995. "Openings in the Wall: Transnational Migrants, Labor Unions, and U.S. Immigration Policy." *International Organization* 49(2):285–313.

Harrison, B. 1994. *Lean and Mean: The Changing Landscape of Corporate Power in the Age of Flexibility*. New York: Basic Books.

Harrison, B., and B. Bluestone. 1990. "Wage Polarization in the U.S. and the Flexibility Debate." *Cambridge Journal of Economics* 14: 351–73.

Hollifield, J. 1992. *Immigrants, Markets, and States: The Political Economy of Postwar Europe*. Cambridge: Harvard University Press.

———. 1998. "Ideas, Institutions and Civil Society: On the Limits of Immigration Control in France." Paper presented at the Winter Workshop of the Comparative Immigration and Integration Program, University of California, San Diego. February 20.

Hyman, R. 1994. "Industrial Relations in Western Europe: An Era of Ambiguity?" *Industrial Relations* 33(1):1–24.

INSEE. 1996. *Annuaire Statistique de la France*. Paris: Institut National de la Statistique et des Etudes Economiques.

———. 1997. *Les Immigrés en France*. Paris: INSEE.

Ireland, P. 1994. *The Policy Challenge of Ethnic Diversity: Immigration Politics in France and Switzerland*. Cambridge: Harvard University Press.

Istituto Richerche Economiche e Sociale. 1997. "Case Study on the Prevention of Racial Discrimination and Xenophobia and the Promotion of Equal Treatment in the Workplace, Italy." Working Paper No. WP/97/42. Dublin: European Foundation for the Improvement of Living and Working Conditions.

Izquierdo Escribano, A. 1992. *La Inmigración en España 1980–1990*. Madrid: Editorial Trotta.

Jacoby, S., ed. 1995. *The Workers of Nations: Industrial Relations in a Global Economy*. New York: Oxford University Press.

Jimeno, J., and L. Toharia. 1994. *Unemployment and Labor Market Flexibility: Spain*. Geneva: International Labour Office.

Keohane, R. O., and S. Hoffman. 1991. *The New European Community*. Boulder, Colo.: Westview Press.

Kesselman, M., and G. Groux. 1984. *The French Workers' Movement: Economic Crisis and Political Change*. London: George Allen and Unwin.

Kritz, M., C. Keely, and S. Tomasi, eds. 1981. *Global Trends in Migration: Theory and Research on International Population Movements*. New York: Center for Migration Studies.

Kritz, M., L. L. Lim, and H. Zlotnik. 1992. *International Migration System: A Global Approach*. Oxford: Clarendon Press.

Labor Immigrant Organizing Network. 1999. "Talking Points on Employer Sanctions." Report prepared by LION, August 20, Alameda, Calif.

Lange, P., and K. Scruggs. 1998. "Where Have All the Members Gone? Union Density in the Era of Globalization." Working Paper 1.63. Center for German and European Studies, University of California, Berkeley.

Lee, K. 1998. *Huddled Masses, Muddled Laws: Why Contemporary Immigration Policy Fails to Reflect Public Opinion*. Westport, Conn.: Praeger.

Lindquist, D. 2000. "Call to Legalize Workers Gives Mexicans Hope." *San Diego Union Tribune*, May 29.

Locke, R., T. Kochan, and M. Piore, eds. 1995. *Employment Relations in a Changing World Economy*. Cambridge: The MIT Press.

López, A. F., and M. Bonmatí. 1997. Opening presentation. *La Seguridad Social de los Migrantes y el papel de las Organizaciones Sindicales en los estados miembros de la Unión Europea*. Madrid: Publícaciones Unión. January.

Lucio, M. M., and P. Blyton. 1995. "Constructing the Post Fordist State? The Politics of Labor Market Flexibility in Spain." *West European Politics*. 18(2): 340–60.

Marie, C. V. 1994. "From the Campaign against Illegal Migration to the Campaign against Illegal Work." *The American Academy of Political and Social Science* (*AAPSS*) 534: 118–32.

Martin, P. 1998. "The Endless Debate: Immigration and U.S. Agriculture." In *The Debate in the United States over Immigration*, edited by P. Duignan and L. Gann. Stanford, Calif.: Hoover Institution.

——. 2000. "Guest Worker Programs for the 21st Century." Center for Immigration Studies Backgrounder. "Backgrounder" is a series put out by the Center for Immigration Studies (CIS), Washington, D.C.

Martinez, L. M., and P. Blyton. 1995. "Constructing the Post-Fordist State? The Politics of Labor Market Flexibility in Spain." *West European Politics* 18(2):340–60.

Migration News Sheet. 1999. Southern Europe. Vol. 11. http://migration.ucdavis.edu.

Miles, R., and D. Thranhardt, eds. 1995. *Migration and European Integration: The Dynamics of Inclusion and Exclusion*. London: Print Publishers.

Milkman, R., ed. 2000. *Organizing Immigrants: The Challenge for Unions in Contemporary California*. Ithaca, N.Y.: Cornell University Press.

Miller, M. 1981. *Foreign Workers in Western Europe: An Emerging Political Force*. New York: Praeger.

Milner, H. 1988. *Resisting Protectionism*. Princeton: Princeton University Press.

Ministry of Labor and Social Affairs. 1994. *Plan for the Social Integration of Immigrants*. Madrid: Ministry of Labor and Social Affairs.

——. 1996a. *Migration Annual*. Madrid: Ministry of Labor and Social Affairs.

——. 1996b. *Boletín Estadístico de Datos Básicos*. No. 24. Madrid: Ministry of Labor and Social Affairs.

——. 1997. *Migration Annual*. Madrid: Ministry of Labor and Social Affairs.

Ness, I. 1998. "Organizing Immigrant Communities: UNITE's Workers' Center Strategy." In *Organizing to Win*, edited by K. Bronfenbrenner, S. Friedman, R. W. Hurd, R. A. Oswald, and R. L. Seeber. Ithaca, N.Y.: ILR Press.

Nissen, B. 1999. *Which Direction for Organized Labor?* Detroit: Wayne State University Press.

Ochoa de Michelena, C. 1993. "La Inmigración Hacia España de los Naturales de Países Terceros a la CEE: Un Nuevo Fenómeno." *Política y Sociedad* 12:97–120.

OECD. 1996a. *OECD Economic Survey, Spain*. Paris: OECD.

——. 1996b. *Trends in International Migration*. Paris: OECD.

——. 1997a. *OECD Economic Survey, Italy*. Paris: OECD.

——. 1997b. *OECD Economic Survey, France*. Paris: OECD.

——. 1997c. *SMEs and Globalization*. Paris: OECD.

——. 1999. *Trends in International Migration*. Paris: OECD.

Ohmae, K. 1990. *The Borderless World: Power and Strategy in the Interlinked Economy*. New York: Harper Perennial.

——. 1996. *The End of the Nation State*. New York: Free Press Paperbacks.

Perlmutter, T. 1996. "Immigration Politics Italian Style: The Paradoxical Behavior of Mainstream and Populist Parties." *South European Society and Politics* 1(2):229–52.

Piore, M. 1979. *Birds of Passage: Migrant Labor in Industrial Societies*. Cambridge: Cambridge University Press.

Piore, M., and C. Sabel. 1984. *The Second Industrial Divide: Possibilities for Prosperity*. New York: Basic Books.

Portes, A. 1983. "International Labor Migration and National Development." In *U.S. Immigration and Refugee Policy*, edited by M. Kritz. Lexington, Mass.: Lexington Books.

Puente, T., and S. Franklin. 2000. "Labor Offers Support to Immigrant Amnesty." *Chicago Tribune*, June 5.

Pugliese, E. 1996. "Italy between Emigration and Immigration and the Problems of Citizenship." In *Citizenship, Nationality and Migration in Europe*, edited by D. Cesarani and M. Fulbrook. London: Routledge.

Pumares Fernándes, P. 1996. *La Integración de los Inmigrantes Marroquies: Familias Marroquies en la Comunidad de Madrid*. Barcelona: Fundación la Caixa.

Regini, M., ed. 1992. *The Future of Labour Movements*. London: Sage.

——. 1995. *Uncertain Boundaries: The Social and Political Construction of European Economies*. Cambridge: Cambridge University Press.

Reuters. 1997. Wire Service, December 3.

Rogowski, R. 1989. *Commerce and Coalitions*. Princeton: Princeton University Press.

Sassen, S. 1988. *The Mobility of Capital and Labor*. Cambridge: Cambridge University Press.

Schain, M. 1994. "Ordinary Politics: Immigrants, Direct Action, and the Political Process in France" *French Politics & Society* 12(2/3):65–81.

Schmidley, A. D., and J. G. Robinson. 1998. "How Well Does the Current Population Survey Measure the Foreign Born Population in the U.S.?" U.S. Census Bureau, Population Division Working Paper No. 22.

Schmitter, B. E. 1981. "Trade Unions and Immigration Politics in West Germany and Switzerland." *Politics and Society* 10(3):317–34.

Schneider, F., and D. Enste. 2000. "Shadow Economies: Sizes, Causes, and Consequences." *Journal of Economic Literature* 38(1):77–114.

Senato della Repubblica, XIII Legislatura. 1998. "Disciplina dell'immigrazione e norme sulla condizione dello straniero." (Text of 1998 Immigration law)

Sengenberger, W., G. Loveman, and M. J. Piore. 1990. *The Re-emergence of Small Enterprises: Industrial Restructuring in Industrialized Countries*. Geneva: International Institute for Labour Studies.

Solé, C. 1997. "Inmigración y Mercado de Trabajo." Conference paper. Fundación La Caixa–Instituto Universitario Ortega y Gasset. Madrid. October 16.

Theys, M. 1992. "The Schengen Agreements on Freedom of Movement for Persons in the European Union." Brussels: Europe Agency.

Thomas, J. J. 1992. *Informal Economic Activity*. Ann Arbor: University of Michigan Press.

Thranhardt, D. 1992. *Europe—A New Immigration Continent*. Hamburg: Lit Verlag.

Traxler, F. 1991. "The Logic of Employers' Collective Action." In *Employers' Associations in Europe*, edited by D. Sadowski and O. Jacobi. Baden-Baden, Germany: Nomos Verlagsgesellschaft.

UGT. 1993. "UGT e Inmigración: Un Programa Sindical." Resolución y documento base VI Comite Confederal. (Documentation and resolutions adopted by the Confederal Committee on Social Action)

——. 1996. Secretariá Acción Social Confederal. Área de Migraciones. "Jornada de

Trabajo Sobre el Nuevo Reglamento de la Ley Organica 7/1985, de 1 de Julio sobre los Derechos y Libertades de los Extranjeros en España." (Information packet on 1985 LOE)

Ulman, L., B. Eichengreen, and W. T. Dickens, eds. 1993. *Labor and an Integrated Europe*. Washington, D.C.: The Brookings Institution.

U.S. Department of Justice. 2000. *1998 Statistical Yearbook of the Immigration and Naturalization Service*.

Venturini, A. 1988. "An Interpretation of Mediterranean Migration." *Labour* 2(2):125–54.

——. 1991. "Italy in the Context of European Migration." *Regional Development Dialogue* 12(3):93–112.

Visser, J. 1991. "Trends in Union Membership." In OECD, *Employment Outlook*. Paris: OECD.

Wallerstein, M. 1989. "Centralized Bargaining and Wage Restraint." Working Paper, no. 166. Institute of Industrial Relations, University of California, Los Angeles.

Western, B. 1997. *Between Class and Market: Postwar Unionization in the Capitalist Democracies*. Princeton: Princeton University Press.

Wever, K. 1998. "International Labor Revitalization: Enlarging the Playing Field." *Industrial Relations* 37(3):388–407.

Withol de Wenden, C. 1988. "Trade Unions, Islam, and Immigration." *Economic and Industrial Democracy* 9:65–82.

Wood, S. 1989. *The Transformation of Work? Skill, Flexibility, and the Labour Process*. London: Unwin Hyman.

Index

AFL-CIO, 3, 13, 145–147, 152–159, 164–166

Amnesty, 24–25, 74, 78–79, 143
  France and, 43–44, 46, 48, 118
  Italy and, 35–41, 124, 140–141
  Spain and, 29–32, 115
  United States and, 150, 166–167

Amsterdam Treaty (1997), 59, 106, 127, 131, 135

Auroux Laws (1982), 91

Barre, Raymond, 45–46
Bracero Program, 149, 162
Brochmann, Grete, 138

Chavez-Thompson, Linda, 157–158
Chemouil, Gérard, 57–58, 65
Chevènement Law (1998), 49, 120
Chirac, Jacques, 45–48, 119
Comisiones Obreras (CCOO), 58, 60, 66–70, 111
  Centro de Información para Trabajadores Extranjeros (CITE) and, 67–68, 116

Confederación Española de Organizaciones Empresariales (CEOE), 81, 90, 97, 102

Confédération Française Démocratique du Travail (CFDT), 56, 58, 65–66, 113, 116–121

Confédération Générale du Travail (CGT), 1, 54, 56–58, 61, 64–65, 113, 116–121

Confederazione Generale Italiana del Lavoro (CGIL), 64, 70–73, 122
  Coordinamento Immigrati and, 71
  Ufficio Straneri and, 70

Confederazione Italiana Sindicati Lavoratori (CISL), 12, 57, 64, 70–73
  Associazione Nazionale oltre le Frontiere (ANOLF) and, 71–73

Confindustria, 98

Conseil National de Patronat Français (CNPF), 10, 82, 85, 87–88, 91, 97
  Huvelin, Paul and, 87–88

Debré Law (1997), 48
Debs, Eugene, 2
Dini Decree (1996), 38, 104, 123–124

179

Author Biography

Julie R. Watts received her Ph.D. in political science from New York University and her undergraduate degree from Northwestern University. Her research focuses how labor union leaders and employers form their immigration policy preferences and how these groups influence immigration policy. She also examines the effects of regional integration on immigration policy. Her work has been published in *Policy Studies Journal* (Winter 1998), *South European Society and Politics* (Winter 1998), and *Population Research and Policy Review* (Spring 2001).